RUSSIAN LACQUER, LEGENDS and FAIRY TALES

The painting shown on the jacket depicts scenes from *Voron Voronovich* — The Raven. This is a tale about an old man and his wife, whose three daughters are the most beautiful maidens in the realm. The eldest daughter marries the Sun; the middle daughter marries the Moon; the youngest daughter marries a Raven. The wall panel, painted in Palekh, is shown actual size.

RUSSIAN LACQUER, LEGENDS and FAIRY TALES

Lucy Maxym

This book is dedicated

To Nadia — In memory of shared joys and sorrows

To Stephen — without whose devotion and constant support nothing would have been possible.

To my children and grandchildren — with love.

First Printing July, 1981
Second Printing December, 1981
Third Printing December, 1982
Fourth Printing January, 1984
Fifth Printing November, 1984

Inquiries should be addressed to: Siamese Imports Co., Inc., 148 Plandome Road, Manhasset, N.Y. 11030.

Library of Congress Cataloging in Publication Data

Maxym, Lucy.
    Russian lacquer, legends and fairy tales.

    1. Lacquer and lacquering—Russian S.F.S.R.
2. Legends, Russian. 3. Fairy tales, Russian.
4. Miniature painting, Russian. I. Title.
NK9900.7.S652R84   745.7'2   81-51492
ISBN 0-940202-01-8   AACR2

Printed in United States of America

CONTENTS

Preface 6

Introduction 8
    How the Pâpier-Maché articles are made 9
    A word about "Borders" 10
    The Villages: Fedoskino 10
                   Palekh 11
                   Kholui 12
                   Mstera 12

Legends and Fairy Tales
    Tsar Saltan 13
    Konok Garbunok — The Humpbacked Pony 19
    Vasilisa the Beautiful 26
    The Firebird, Tsarevich Ivan and the Gray Wolf . . . 32
    Rusalka 37
    General Toptiggin 39
    The Frog Princess 40
    The Fisherman and the Magic Fish 45
    The Old Man and the Hares 47
    Alyonushka 48
    Snegurochka — The Snowmaiden 51
    Morozko — Father Frost and the Maiden 55
    Prince Igor 57
    Sadko 58
    The Girl with the Golden Hair 61
    The Stone Flower 62
    The Golden Cockerel — Le Coq d'Or 64
    The Merchant-Peddlers 67
    Ruslan and Ludmilla 68

Full Page Plates
    The Epic of Prince Igor, Kholui 71
    Cathedrals and Monasteries, Kholui 72
    "The Small Miracles" of Palekh 73
    Masterpieces from Mstera 74
    Russian Paintings, Fedoskino 76
    Troikas 77
    Village Life 78

Listing of Distinguished Miniature Painters 79

Preface

I am tempted to start this preface with "Once upon a time . . . "

It is difficult to think that my first glimpse of a Russian lacquer box was but fifteen years ago. It seems that they have been a part of my life for much longer than that.

A dear friend of ours who lived in Philadelphia gave my husband and me the use of her apartment for a parents' week-end at nearby Swarthmore College, where our son was a student.

In this apartment, full of lovely works of art, my eye was caught by a gleaming little black lacquer box on the coffee table. I had never seen anything like it, and found it utterly charming. That is how my love affair with Russian lacquer miniatures started.

For many years, my sister and I had been involved in our own thriving business which supplied antiques, handicrafts and lacquerware from all over the world to the wholesale gift trade. Our business started with imports from Thailand, which was still called Siam then — hence our name: Siamese Imports Co.

After my Philadelphia week-end and an enthusiastic description of the enchanting little box to my sister, we immediately set about trying to find out everything we could concerning this art and whether it would be possible for us to import the lacquer miniatures to the United States.

And so, a chance encounter with a little lacquer box resulted in an interesting new facet of our business.

After exchanges of correspondence and receipt of numerous samples, each of which was more fascinating than the last, we introduced the lacquer boxes to the American market. The acceptance was instantaneous.

It was at this point that I realized that it was probably of prime importance for me to learn the Russian language if I were to continue this business in a serious fashion. I must admit that this was one of the most difficult things that I have ever had to do! However, I am thankful that I did follow through on this, for I found that even the halting Russian which was all that I could manage at the time I made my first trip to the Soviet Union was of great importance.

Since that first trip, made shortly after my dear sister's untimely death in 1971, I have made numerous trips to Moscow and to the villages themselves, where I had the opportunity to observe the incredible talent abounding there, to watch the artists at work, and to meet and talk with the people involved in the production of these small miracles. My affection for these people and my appreciation of their work has grown with each succeeding visit.

Within a short time after the introduction of these miniatures to the American market, the growth of interest was tremendous. There are now scores of knowledgeable and avid collectors throughout the United States.

In my travels to various cities, I am constantly asked questions concerning the lacquer articles. There is great interest both in the details of their production as well as in the subject matter contained in the paintings. Since there is almost nothing available in English to satisfy this curiosity, this book is an attempt to answer these questions.

It is of course impossible to include all the Russian fairy tales, songs, legends, operas and ballets. Therefore, the stories in this book consist of those which are the inspiration for a great majority of the paintings done by the lacquer miniaturists. Because fairy tales and legends are handed down from generation to generation, there may be different versions of a story, depending upon what source is used. It is quite difficult to find an "authentic" version of a particular tale, aside from the works of established authors such as Pushkin or Lermontov. A good example of the dilemma facing one with regard to the fairy tales can be illustrated as follows:

In one version of Snegurochka, the childless couple fashion a snowmaiden out of snow in the forest and she comes to life before their eyes. In another version Snegurochka is the daughter of Spring and Winter, and appears to them when they come out of their cottage one frosty morning announcing, "I have come to be your daughter".

I have tried to include those versions of the stories which are the most consistent with the subject matter used by the artists on their boxes. I am deeply grateful to V/O Novoexport for providing translations of some stories which I could not have obtained otherwise.

I wish to take this opportunity to thank the Directors of V/O Novoexport, and the community of artists in each of the villages for the warmth, cooperation and hospitality extended to me during my visits to the Soviet Union. I want to mention particularly, in Palekh, the Chairman of the Board of the Palekh Organization of the Union of Artists A.D. Kochupalov, Director A.U. Kovalev, Chief Artist, R.L. Belousev, and Z.A. Khokhov; in Kholui, Director A.A. Kamorin, Chief Artist B.K. Novoselev, and E.M. Filippov; in Fedoskino, Director N.N. Sedov, Chief Artist Y.V. Gussev, and Valentina Aldoshkina; and in Mstera, Director N.V. Medvedev and Chief Artist N.I. Shishakov.

These men and women are justifiably proud of their achievements and have always made me feel that they are particularly pleased with the acceptance and appreciation of their work in the United States. They have done much to increase my personal knowledge of this art.

I wish also to express my love and appreciation to my colleagues and associates, who have worked with me for so many years and whose faith and loyalty have made it possible to carry on a most interesting enterprise: Paul Olson, Jeri Schachter and Leroy Williams, who take such impeccable care of the business at hand; Amy Connors, our lovely ray of sunshine, whose unfailing enthusiasm and optimism warms us all; dear Willie Mercer, who has made it possible for me to leave my family and home for the necessary trips abroad; and Ann Gordon, whose creativity and solid professionalism have been of inestimable value. Ann's and my experiences abroad together, many of which have been hilarious, could well provide sufficient material for still another book!

Among the people who have been involved in the production of this book with me, I would especially like to thank Bruce Toole, who so ably coordinated the work connected with the photography, color separation, lay-out and printing.

Many of the articles shown are from private collections. My sincere thanks to the collectors who have so graciously allowed me to have their lacquer miniatures photographed for inclusion in this book.

Finally, I want to thank my family for being so enthusiastically supportive and interested in my career and making it possible for me to pursue the opportunities which came my way.

L.M.

Manhasset, New York
May, 1981

Introduction

The art of miniature painting on pâpier-maché articles originated in Russia in the late eighteenth century in the village of Danilkovo, not far from Moscow. It was then adopted in the neighboring village of Fedoskino, where it still thrives.

The most precious and fascinating element of Russian lacquer art is of course the handpainted miniature decoration. In this art of miniature painting there is no mechanization possible. On the contrary, every miniature is the product of an inspired process of individual creation, which lends the finished article its unique quality.

A whole world of complex and rich artistic images unfold before our eyes when we look at the paintings. We see multi-figure compositions, delicately executed miniature portraits, fascinating Russian landscapes showing the vivid beauty of rivers, meadows and forests, delicate renderings of birds and flowers, and the magnificent heritage of ancient Russian architecture with its golden-domed churches and crenelated walls and towers.

Extremely fine brushes are used. Each artist makes his own brushes from whatever material he feels is best suited for a specific task. A favorite type of brush is made from sable or the hair taken from the tail of a squirrel.

When delicate and sensitive details are being painted, the piece is placed under a large high-intensity magnifying glass, for each stroke of the brush or a line, no matter how tiny, must be accurate and emotionally expressive. When working on a piece which is perhaps only a few square centimeters in area upon which a whole story unfolds, the entire painting is done under a magnifying glass. The concentration necessary when working on the tiny miniatures is enormous; therefore the artist can paint for only short periods of time on these.

Trees, foliage, scenery, the intricate decorative elements of architectural monuments, tiny figures of people at work or at play, the lovely ornamentation of their garments are all painted in painstaking detail in the small space of the miniature.

In each of the villages of Fedoskino, Palekh, Kholui and Mstera where this work now flourishes, there are approximately 175 to 250 artists working at a given time. In addition to the artists themselves, there are numerous people involved in the preparation and finishing of the articles.

Each of the villages has a special school where young people, under the guidance of experienced masters, learn the aesthetics of all art as well as the techniques of this particular art.

Young artists apply for admission from all parts of the country. There are ten to fifteen times as many applicants for each opening as the schools can accept. After a strict review of their work and aptitude by the entrance committees, composed of established artists, approximately 20 to 25 applicants are admitted yearly to each school.

The four year courses are thorough. The young artists go through rigid training and have to prove their talent before they are allowed to graduate and become members of the community of miniature painters in each village.

There are several catagories of work produced. The first is that of the masters, who create unique pieces which are destined for Museums throughout their country. We are fortunate indeed to be able to obtain a limited number of these works for our collectors in the United States each year.

Secondly, an artist can paint a particular composition in a "limited edition" of perhaps five to twenty pieces over a period of time. In this case, it is only the original painter who will produce this particular work.

There is also a third catagory in which a composition is created by an artist which, after submission to a review committee consisting of established masters, can be made available to all the other artists to use if they wish.

Whether it is part of a "limited edition" or a design which is produced in large quantities, each box is painted as a separate entity. One can compare one box with another, seemingly of the same design, and find that each one is quite different and expresses the mood and personality of the artist who painted it.

The carefully checked pieces are given to the joiners.

The outside is covered with black lacquer; the inside with red lacquer.

8

How the Pâpier-Maché Articles Are Made

The basic material for making the pâpier-maché articles is cardboard. Thin sheets of this material are sliced on a special machine to specific sizes, glued and pressed together.

While they are still wet with glue, they are wrapped around various forms and pressed into long tubes of differing shapes which will make the boxes. The forms can be rectangular, square, round, or cylindrical.

When the material is dry, it is placed in a hot linseed oil bath for approximately 20 to 25 minutes, after which it is put into a special airtight electrical "oven" for drying. The drying process gradually takes the material from room temperature up to about 100° C. and back again to room temperature over a period of 30 days. This is a complicated procedure that requires special skill on the part of the people overseeing it.

When the pieces are taken out of the ovens, they are sliced with a circular saw into the actual sizes of the required boxes and given over to the joiners, who make up the required shapes with tops and bottoms which have been processed separately. Joints, hinge-plates and sometimes locks are skillfully inserted at this point. These must be attached most carefully since papier-mache is a material which is quite difficult to work with for these purposes. An experienced joiner must also be proficient at working with metal.

The semi-finished pieces are now covered with a black paste made up of various ingredients. Three coats of this paste are applied; after each coat the piece is placed in an oven to dry for one day at 90° C.

The article is then cleaned and polished to a smooth finish with a fine sanding cloth.

Now the lacquering begins. The outside of the box is covered two or three times with a black lacquer and dried for a day after each coat. Then the inside is covered with two to three coats of red lacquer and again dried for a day after each coat.

Next the box is covered with several coats of clear lacquer, inside and out, and again dried after each coat.

At this point, the preparation for painting is finished and the piece is given to the artist.

When the artist gets the box, the design is outlined on the cover, after which a coating of zinc or titanium is placed on it, and the actual painting commences. The colors are applied in strict succession.

When the painting is finished, the artist begins the gold work. Gold leaf is carefully crushed and ground by hand. After it is applied, the gold must be polished to give it the necessary glow. This is done with a wolf's tooth, which has a remarkably smooth surface.

The pieces are dried in "ovens".

The artist makes several sketches in preparation for painting on the box.

After the box is completed, it is given to the polishing department, where it goes through additional polishing and lacquering stages, all painstakingly done by hand with cloths of increasing fineness.

From start to finish, excluding the time spent by the artist for the actual painting, it takes from a minimum of 45 days to sometimes as much as 60 days to complete the drying, polishing and lacquering processes for the boxes, plates and plaques.

The above proceedures are followed, with slight variations, in all four villages.

The question has often been posed as to why pâpier-maché is used for the articles rather than wood, which, after all, is readily available in Russia. There is a very good reason. After the complicated treatment of the pâpier-maché described above, the result is an article which will not be affected by changing atmospheric conditions, as is the case with even well seasoned wood. What a tragedy it would be if a box which can take over a year to paint would split when taken from the atmosphere in which it was created to a place continents away. In actuality then, the pâpier-maché gives us an article that will neither warp, crack nor craze, and a smooth base for the painting which even the finest wood cannot achieve.

A Word About "Borders"

The last step before final lacquering on all the Palekh boxes, most of the Kholui boxes, and the most important of the Mstera boxes is the painting of the graphic ornament which forms a border around the four sides of the box or on the top edges. In the case of some of the more intricate and very special boxes, there are borders on both the tops and the sides. Pure gold leaf is used to paint these borders, and, in some cases, a touch of silver, red, or other color is used as well to enhance the overall effect.

These borders continue to amaze me. I have been looking at them and examining them for almost fifteen years, and I have yet to find a duplication of any one of these free-hand border designs. It is inconceivable to me that there are so many variations possible!

On one of my first visits to the studios in Palekh, I watched a young artist putting the final few flourishes on the side border of a particularly intricate and beautiful box. The top border was already finished, and she told me that she had been working on this box, on and off, for over eight months and planned to finish it that very day.

The box stood on the table before her under a large magnifying glass. The young woman rested her arm, between the elbow and the wrist, on a narrow wooden arm rest. She was using a brush which seemed to have no more than one or two hairs in it.

I held my breath until the last tiny line was painted, and we both, almost as one, breathed a sigh of relief when she was done. I could not resist asking her what she would have done if her hand had slipped, ruining eight months' work. She had a very short, simple and quick answer: "I would have killed myself!"

We laughed, and I congratulated her on the exquisite beauty of the little box she had just finished.

The Village of Fedoskino

The Villages

Fedoskino

During the nineteenth century, Fedoskino miniature art took much of its inspiration from classical Russian painting, as well as from ancient Russian engravings and popular paintings. One example is "Morning in the Woods," a scene showing a bear and her cubs in the early morning mists of the forest. (see page 76) Another is "The Rooks are Returning," depicting the first birds of Spring returning while the snow is still on the ground and the trees are bare. These paintings hang in the Tretyakov Gallery in Moscow. Still another subject is "The Boyar's Wedding," a magnificent painting by Makovsky which is now part of the Marjorie Merryweather Post collection housed in the Hillwood Museum in Washington. (see page 76)

The Fedoskino artists also paint village scenes and folk festivals. They often portray scenes of popular festivities and dancers in national costumes shown in the measured poses of age-old country dances. One of the favorite and constantly recurring subjects from Fedoskino is the careening Troika, "The Flying Troika" as Gogol called it.

In addition to these subjects, Fedoskino masters are inspired by the heritage of untold numbers of fairy tales, songs and legends.

Fedoskino artists use very thinly diluted oil paints, which are applied in several layers. Often before painting a miniature, parts of the background are coated with a sheet of pure gold or silver leaf which remains visible through the translucent layers of paint, lending an unusually effective decorative appearance to the completed miniature. This technique is known as "translucent painting." Thanks to this method, the coachman's *caftan* or a girl's gaily colored shawl and *sarafan* seem to light up and glow, a silvery sparkle is emitted in a snowy scene, the sunset shines like gold, and tiny little windows in far-off huts glow with light from within.

Palekh

There are few art lovers who have not heard of Palekh. Its art has been called "a small miracle." Lacquered miniatures, as bright as the feathers of the legendary Firebird, originate here, taking the inspired poetic art of this village to the far corners of the world.

Palekh is an unusual village, a bit of ancient Russia in which the past and the present co-exist. Log houses with intricately carved lattices stand opposite modern brick buildings. There are street pumps, and the crowing of roosters can be heard above whatever traffic there is. Each house stands among poplars, acacias and rowan trees. Here the soft hues of the Russian countryside are both a part of everyday village life and an endless source of inspiration for the artists.

Icons found in old Russian churches attest to the glory of the painters of Palekh, who were famed for their Icon painting in ancient times. The secrets of this art were handed down from father to son.

After 1918, the demand for Icons stopped and the artists turned their efforts toward the making of miniature boxes, jewelry and panels.

Palekh artists do not use oil paints. They use tempera paints with an egg yolk base. This technique of mixing colors with egg yolk was used in ancient times by the Palekh Icon painters and is continued in the work done there today. The Palekh palette is remarkable for its gay colors and clean bright hues. The drawing is laconic and expressive. The expressiveness is achieved by the plasticity of every individual line, every contour, the rhythmic wealth of the compositions. On Palekh miniatures, just as in ancient Russian Icon paintings, people have somewhat elongated proportions, their movements are measured and graceful and they take the viewer into a realm of history, legend and song. To emphasize and single out individual forms, human figures, or groups of people, the painter uses filigree shading or golden rimming, similar to gold inlaid patterns.

Palekh subjects sometimes unfold in succession. One miniature may depict a number of scenes occurring consecutively in time and space. The same character or group of characters may recur in a composition several times. (see page 70) The Palekh masters often use all of the sides of a box, as well as the top, to unfold the subject as a successive series of interconnected compositions. (see page 73)

Great professional mastery of their medium, fascinating subject material, sensitive treatment of details, artistic inspiration and beauty of colors make every Palekh piece a work of art which gives its viewer great aesthetic pleasure.

Palekh painters create miniatures on historic and contemporary themes. They, as well as the artists of the other villages, are strongly inspired by the works of the great Russian poets and authors such as Pushkin, Lermontov, Nekrassov, Gorky, Mayakovsky and Bazhov, as well as by Russian folk songs, *bylinas* (legends), operas and ballets. Some of the operas and ballets are, of course, based on the works of the self-same authors. Fairy tales hold a particularly conspicuous place among the subject matter used. Other favorite themes are fierce battles, the ubiquitous troika, hunts, country dances, and country occupations such as picking mushrooms, picking berries, fishing and walking in the forest. Many boxes depict the famous "Palekh Horses," those fiery steeds invariable shown rearing up in a frenzy of mythological splendor, mounted by Knights in magnificent flowing cloaks or coats of mail.

A magnifying glass is used when painting delicate details.

Kholui

Kholui miniatures occupy an intermediate place between Fedoskino and Palekh art. They have much of the spontaneity and true-to-life veracity in depicting scenes of life characteristic of Fedoskino and, at the same time, many fantastic and exquisite qualities uniquely their own. Kholui masters paint miniatures in which the unity of place, time and action is preserved, but they also produce several independently treated subject scenes united in one composition to convey a successive occurrence of events in time.

Many Kholui paintings are intensely romantic and lyrical, with great emotional appeal. The dominant feeling that permeates these artists' work appears to be one of specific, exalted joy. Their art seems to say to the spectator, "Look — isn't this beautiful!"

Black lacquer is used as a background, as in the other villages. A very few boxes are painted on red lacquer, but these are quite rare and greatly prized. In Kholui works, in contrast to Palekh, people have more realistic proportions. Great attention is given to nature and landscape, particularly that of the village of Kholui itself, which is located on both banks of the picturesque Teza river. Many of the boxes depict the tranquil beauty surrounding the village.

The Teza is a typical small river in central Russia. During the spring high water season, the river spreads over a vast area, flooding its banks and coming to the very edge of the village and sometimes into the houses and the studios where the painting is done. During these times, everyone uses little boats for transportation.

This yearly flooding lends a special color to the spring landscape of Kholui, and its miniature painters are fond of depicting floods of the Teza and views of their native village in spring.

As do the artists of all the villages, Kholui masters choose diverse subjects for their work: fairy tales, *bylinas*, contemporary themes and, of course, the beloved poems and stories of their giants of literature, with which every Russian seems to be intimately familiar from childhood on. Kholui artists were the first to paint miniatures dedicated to the conquest of space. The hero cosmonauts are presented in fairy tale scenes, riding their majestic steeds higher and higher into the sky and beyond, into unknown stellar worlds.

Mstera

Mstera miniatures differ considerably from those of the other villages. Their miniatures are characteristically done in pale tones, usually on an ivory background.

The village of Mstera is situated in the center of what was formerly the Vladimir-Suzdal province, at the confluence of the Msterka and Klyazma rivers, the latter being a tributary of the Oka.

For centuries, Mstera painters produced Icons of extraordinary quality.

The scenes in Mstera miniatures are the river floodlands, boundless fields, picturesque villages, far-away blue forests. Landscape holds a dominant place in the Mstera miniatures. This is not the individual landscape motif almost invariably present in Palekh and Kholui works, but a general light and airy landscape, known as "plein-air". Nor is it a 19th-20th century landscape resembling classical Russian painting to be met with in Fedoskino miniatures, but a fairy tale scenery with blue rivers, ornamental huts and pink or lilac hills, which has come down to the Mstera miniature from the heritage of ancient Russian painting. Human figures seem to dissolve into the landscape.

As a rule, Mstera miniatures are painted on only the cover of a box; rarely is a box painted on all sides, but when it is it is exquisite. And almost invariably, the miniature is framed with a thin golden ornament made of vegetable color. On the most important pieces, pure gold is used for the ornamental borders.

Within the limits of the conventionalities characteristic of Mstera painting, artists produce compositions on a variety of themes: fairy tales and songs, historical events, floral designs, heroic battle compositions, and lyrical renderings of young people in love, meeting in those places where they were wont to meet for generations — at the village well, in the forest picking mushrooms and berries, on the street near their homes, at festivals and holiday fairs.

Some of the finest examples of Mstera art contain, within the limits of a single box, incredibly detailed battle scenes with apparently unending scores of men and horses, complicated compositions depicting elaborate court scenes and, in the case of one box shown in this book, seemingly all the events in the life of Ivan the Great, within the confines of the top of one small box. (see page 75)

Life goes on quietly in these four small villages. These are places where old masters lived, and their heritage called to life a new art which is linked strongly to its roots.

In the colors and silhouettes, the linear patterns and the very character of the contemporary miniature paintings, we hear the echoes of the great ancient painters, book illustrators and Icon painters. Today's young masters study the ancient art forms, trying to penetrate deep into their meanings to learn the mystery of the beauty of color and the expressiveness of line.

Russian lacquer miniature painting is an important and unique 20th century art form. It reflects the thoughts and aspirations of the artists, who are appreciative of the beauty of their surroundings, of the sunrise and sunset, of a blossoming tree, of warmth, of love, of peace. Their art is both picturesque and lucid. It asserts life and, therefore, finds its way into the hearts of all people.

The Tale of Tsar Saltan

The Tsar came
into the room where
the three sisters were talking.

Palekh

The poem *Tsar Saltan* is considered to be one of Alexander Pushkin's major works.

Long long ago, in a faraway kingdom, three maidens were sitting under their window late one night, talking idly of what each of them would do if the

Tsar were to take them as wife. The first one said, "I would prepare a feast for all of Christendom."

The second one said, "I would weave fine linens for the whole Tsardom."

"If I were Queen," said the third sister, "I would bear a hero son for our beloved Tsar."

It so happened that Tsar Saltan had been listening behind the window, and after the third sister spoke, he came into the room. Finding the third sister comely and to his liking, he told her that he would marry her. The first sister was to go to the palace and cook, while the second would be the weaver for all in the palace.

The very next evening, the wedding took place, and that same night the Queen conceived a son, while one sister raged in the kitchen and the second wept in envy at her loom.

Shortly thereafter, there was a war, and Tsar Saltan left for the battlefield, admonishing his wife to take good care of herself and their unborn child while he was away.

In due time, the Queen gave birth to a beautiful son, and sent a courier off to her husband with the glad tidings. However, the two sisters and their friend Babarikha the schemer, filled with untold envy of the Queen, killed the Queen's courier and sent another telling the Tsar that the Queen had that night borne "not a son, not a daughter, not a mouse, not a frog, but an unknown little creature."

When Tsar Saltan received this news at the battlefield, he was filled with such anger and wrath that he wanted to hang the courier then and there. However, his good nature prevailed, and he did not do so, but sent back a message to his kingdom that nothing was to be done about his offspring until he returned from the war.

When the courier arrived back in the Kingdom, Babarikha and the two sisters intercepted him before he reached the palace and plied him with drink until he was so drunk that he knew nothing. They then replaced the message which he had brought from the Tsar with another one ordering that the Queen and her baby were to be put into a tarred barrel, and that the barrel was to be rolled off into the ocean.

Since there was no way that the Tsar's order could be disobeyed, the Queen and her babe were put into a barrel and rolled into the ocean. While the Queen wept bitterly inside the barrel, the babe grew bigger and stronger by the minute. When a large wave came over the barrel, the boy beseeched the wave to wash them on to dry land. The wave obeyed, and they found themselves placed very gently on the shore of a craggy island.

Mother and son were now free, but very hungry. Gvidon, who was now a handsome and strong lad, broke a branch off a large oak tree, bent it into a stout bow, took the silken cord from his cross and strung the bow. He made a sharp arrow out of a thin little twig and started out in search of game.

He shot
his arrow into
the hawk and killed him.

Kholui
(Shown actual size)

Just as he reached the sea, he heard a cry and saw a beautiful white swan struggling against a huge black hawk. The swan was churning and lashing the water around her in her efforts to get away from the black bird. Just as the hawk spread his talons and was about to bury his sharp beak into the swan's neck, the young lad shot his arrow into the hawk and killed him, spilling his blood into the sea. With horrifying cries, the hawk fell into the water and drowned.

The white swan swam up to the Prince and told him that he had not killed a hawk at all, but a wicked warlock. She told him that she would serve him always and never forget that he had saved her life.

The swan swam off and the Prince returned to his mother, the Queen. He told her his story, and although he had not come back with any game, nor had they drunk any water, they were so tired that they fell asleep on the shore. The next morning they awoke to see a wondrous walled city before their eyes. Gleaming in the sun were the golden onion domes of many beautiful churches and monasteries. The Queen wondered aloud how this city could appear where there had been nothing the night before. The Prince thought to himself: "I see my swan has been busy!"

The two walked up to the city and throngs of people came to greet them. Bells pealed and a church choir praised God. A splendid court met them and all proclaimed Gvidon as their ruler. Gvidon and his mother went to the white stone palace, which was now to be their home, and lived there very happily.

One day a ship sailed up to the island, and the ship's sailors saw the wondrous sight of the walled city before them, where there had been only a craggy island the last time they had passed it. They were very curious and made fast to the breakwater, wanting to see more. Prince Gvidon made them welcome, fed them fine food and wine and asked them where they were headed. They told him that they were on their way past the Island of Buyan to the Kingdom of Tsar Saltan.

Prince Gvidon asked the merchant sailors to give his greetings to Tsar Saltan and extend his invitation to the Tsar to come and visit him on his island.

After the merchant sailors left his palace and went back to their ship in preparation for sailing on the morrow, the Prince, saddened at the mention of his father, went to the shore and told the swan that he longed to see his father. The swan churned the water all around him, and as he was splashed with the water, he turned into a gnat, flew out to the ship, which was waiting for the dawn to set sail, and hid in a crack in the mast.

When the ship arrived at Saltan's Kingdom, the Tsar made the merchant sailors welcome and asked them to tell him of the lands they had seen and the adventures they had had.

The sailors told Tsar Saltan about the wondrous island and the Prince who had asked them to extend his invitation to the Tsar to visit him. They described the golden-domed churches, and the beautiful palace and gardens where Gvidon lived. The sailors then told the Tsar about another place with golden domes and a large spruce tree beneath which a squirrel sat and sang songs and gnawed at little golden nuts which had kernels of pure emeralds.

Tsar Saltan said that he would dearly like to see Gvidon's walled city for himself. But Babarikha and the two sisters made such fun of the sailors' stories that the Tsar decided not to go.

The gnat, which had flown into the Tsar's palace from the ship, heard all this, and in his rage he stung his aunt in the eye. All the servants tried to catch him, but he calmly flew through the window and back across the sea to his own realm.

Back in his own kingdom, Gvidon sorrowfully walked by the sea, and the swan asked him what was troubling him. He told her the story of the squirrel and the golden nuts which he had heard from the sailors in his father's palace.

Hardly had he returned to his castle when there in the courtyard, under a tall spruce tree, what should he see but a little squirrel, gnawing at a golden nut, taking out the emerald kernel, and placing it upon even piles of golden shells and emerald kernels already on the ground!

Gvidon fashioned a crystal house for the little squirrel and, moreover, had a clerk keep strict count of the nuts: profit for Gvidon; honor for the squirrel!

Some time later, a second ship came to his realm, and again Gvidon welcomed the sailors. When he heard that they too were headed past the Island of Buyan to Tsar Saltan's realm, he asked them to give the Tsar his greetings and bid him come and visit Gvidon.

That evening, Gvidon again went to the sea and met the swan and begged her to make it possible for him to go to his father's realm on the ship. The swan changed him into a fly, and he flew to the ship and made the voyage to the kingdom of Tsar Saltan.

When they arrived, the Tsar made the sailors welcome, fed them food and wine, and asked them what they had seen in their travels.

They recounted the tale of the wondrous walled city on the faraway island, with its golden domed churches, beautiful gardens, and a courtyard where a little squirrel in a crystal house sang songs and gnawed on little golden nuts with emerald kernels. They said that coins were made of the golden shells and beautiful maidens poured the emeralds into caskets which were stored away. Everyone on the island was rich. There were no cottages —only mansions. They related also a story about another island, where they had seen thirty-three heroes rising out from the waves, led by old Chernomor. These handsome young giants, with coats of mail glowing like fire, rose from the sea each morning to guard their island and returned to the waves each evening.

The sailors then relayed Gvidon's greetings to the Tsar and his wish that Saltan would visit him on his island.

Tsar Saltan again marveled at the wondrous tale the sailors told him and decided to visit the island and be Gvidon's guest. However, again the two sisters and Babarikha the schemer made such fun of the stories that the Tsar decided not to go.

Then the fly (Gvidon), enraged at the two sisters and Babarikha for their words, buzzed round and round and landed on his second aunt's left eye. The weaver turned pale and became a crooked old lady. She cried out to catch the fly, but Gvidon flew out through the window and across the sea to his own realm.

When he arrived home, he again went to the sea and walked sadly by the water.

"Why are you so unhappy?" the swan asked.

Gvidon related the story of the thirty-three heroes to her — those handsome young giants with mail of fire, marching behind Chernomor and guarding their island.

"Is that what is troubling you?" asked the swan. "Do you wish to have these knights of the sea in your realm? Then do not sorrow, for they are my brothers, and they will come to you."

Gvidon went off and mounted the tower of his palace. As he gazed out at the sea, suddenly it started to heave about in all directions, and he saw thirty-three knight-heroes, in coats of mail like glowing fire, with silver hair flashing, rise up out of the sea, marching behind bearded Chernomor.

Thirty-three knight-heroes rise up out of the sea, marching behind bearded Chernomor.

Palekh

They came to the palace and told Gvidon that from now on every day without fail they would come up out of the sea to guard his realm.

After some time, a third ship came to the island, and again Gvidon bade the sailors welcome, and when it was time for them to leave told them to give his greetings to Tsar Saltan and ask him to come and visit him.

This time the swan changed Gvidon into a bee, and he flew to the ship as it was setting sail.

Past the Island of Buyan the ship sailed, and when the merchant sailors went ashore in the realm of Tsar Saltan, he bade them be his guests. As they feasted in his palace, he asked them what wonders they had seen in their travels. The merchant sailors told him once more of the wonderful walled city with the golden domed churches and monasteries, the beautiful palace and magnificent gardens, and the courtyard where a magic squirrel gnawed at golden nuts with emerald kernels. They also told him about the thirty-three heroes, who rose up from the sea each day, behind Chernomor, to guard the island of Prince Gvidon. They extended Gvidon's invitation to the Tsar to come to the island and visit him.

At this point, Babarikha interrupted the tales of the sailors and, trying to belittle their stories, said that what they were relating was quite ordinary indeed. What was amazing was that beyond the sea there was a Princess of such beauty that one could not take one's eyes from her. By day, her beauty dimmed the light, by night she lit up the earth. The Moon gleamed under her braid and stars glowed on her brows. When she spoke, it was like a brook murmuring.

"Now that's a marvel!" said the old woman.

The merchant sailors did not wish to argue with Babarikha, so they said nothing. And Gvidon, in his guise of a bee, was raging at the old woman, but he felt sorry for her so he did not sting her in the eyes; instead he settled on her nose, where a huge bump immediately sprang up!

There was a big hue and cry, but the bee could not be caught and flew away out of the window and back to his kingdom.

16

The swan turned into a beautiful Princess.

Mstera

When he returned, Gvidon again walked by the dark-blue sea until the white swan swam up to him. She asked why he was so sad, and Gvidon replied that he was sad because he did not have a wife. The swan asked him whether there was anyone whom he wished to marry, and the Prince told her of the wondrous Princess whom the sailors had described: one who was so fair that it was beyond anyone's ability to tell. Gvidon swore to the swan that he would search the whole world for this Princess, even if it took him to Thrice-Nine Lands away, for it was time for him to marry and only she could be his wife.

The swan replied that it would not be necessary for him to travel beyond the Thrice-Nine Lands, for it was she, the swan, who was the beautiful Princess whom the sailors had described.

Saying this, she beat her wings and flew off above the waves to the shore. There, behind a flowering shrub, she ruffled her plumage, arched her magnificent neck, and turned into the beautiful Princess!

The Moon gleamed beneath her braid and stars glowed on her brows; she was splendid to behold!

Gvidon was overjoyed at the sight of the Princess and clasped her to his breast. He took her to his mother, the Queen, and asked her blessing upon their marriage, which took place that very evening.

Time passed, and another ship came to the island, and again Gvidon asked the merchant sailors to give his greetings to Tsar Saltan and ask him to visit. But this time, being happy with his new bride, he did not leave her to fly away with the ship.

Tsar Saltan called his fleet and set sail for the island.

Palekh

17

In the courtyard was the squirrel, singing a song and gnawing on a golden nut.

Fedoskino

When the ship arrived at the Kingdom of Tsar Saltan, the sailors again regaled him with stories of the wondrous island beyond Buyan. This time he did not listen to the snide remarks of either the sisters or Babarikha. He immediately called his fleet and set sail for the island so that he could see it and visit Prince Gvidon.

In due time, the fleet of Tsar Saltan reached the island. Prince Gvidon met them at the shore. He led Tsar Saltan, the two sisters and Babarikha to the palace, saying nothing.

There were the thirty-three heroes standing guard, and with them Old Chernomor. In the courtyard was the squirrel, singing a song and gnawing on a golden nut, as he took out an emerald kernel and dropped it into a little bag. The courtyard was bestrewn with gold shells and emeralds.

The guests went further, and there stood the beautiful Princess, Gvidon's wife, and at her side was the mother Queen. Tsar Saltan recognized his long-lost Queen and rushed to embrace her.

They sat down to a merry feast. The two sisters and Babarikha scattered into far corners in shame, and it took some time to find them. They confessed to everything that they had done, but Tsar Saltan and his Queen, and Prince Gvidon and his Princess, were so very happy that they forgave them.

Tsar Saltan and his beloved Queen returned to his kingdom; Prince Gvidon and his Princess remained in the beautiful walled city on their island, and all lived happily ever after.

Prince Gvidon met Tsar Saltan at the shore.

Palekh

Konok Garbunok
The Humpbacked Pony

Scenes from Konok Garbunok.　　　　　　　　　　　　　　　　*Mstera*

Once upon a time, in a far away kingdom, there lived a peasant who had three sons: Danilo, the eldest, was sharp as he could be; Gavrilo, the second, was neither dull nor bright; but Ivan, the third, was thought to be a fool!

The three brothers planted wheat and did quite well, until one fine day they found that someone, or something, had trampled down their wheat during the night. This went on night after night. Never had they had such grief before. They thought and thought about what they could do. Finally, the eldest brother said that he would watch during the night to find the culprit.

That night, Danilo took his pitchfork in one hand, an axe in the other, and started his watch. The night was dark and stormy, and he was overcome with fright. So he dove into the nearest haystack and slept the night away.

The next morning, he went back to his house and told his brothers and father a fanciful tale of the terrible night of storm and thunder that he had passed.

The next night, the second brother went to keep watch. The night was beastly cold, so he hid under a neighbor's porch and slept the night away. He too returned the following morning and told a tale of the terrible frosty night he had spent on watch without seeing anything.

The third night, it was Ivan's turn to stand watch.

Night fell and the white moon rose. Ivan sat on the ground, slowly munching at the bread he had brought with him. He counted the bright stars overhead and was lost in thought, when suddenly he heard a mighty neighing sound. He bounded to his feet, and in the field he spied a mare more magnificent than any eye had ever seen and more wonderful than tonque could tell. She was whiter than the whitest snow, with a silken mane in ringlets streaming to the ground, all golden gleaming.

"Oh ho," thought Ivan, "so you're the culprit." And with that he approached her stealthily, seized her tail as in a vice and mounted her, facing her back the better to hold on to her magnificent golden tail.

No matter how hard the mare bucked, he held on. Her eyes blazed with anger and she flew over streams and gullies, rearing and prancing, but all in vain. Ivan held fast.

Finally, spent and trembling, she said:

"Since you sat me, I confess
I am yours now to possess."

The mare told him that now Ivan would have to feed and take care of her. In return, in three days she would bear him two handsome steeds more beautiful than had ever been seen, and a third one which would be quite tiny, with two little humps upon his back, coal black eyes and ears that were a yard long. She told him also that he could sell the two steeds but that he should never part with the little one no matter how dire his need, for he would be the most faithful friend that Ivan could ever have. In the meantime, Ivan would have to find shelter for the mare and leave her there for three days.

19

Ivan found shelter for the mare in a shepherd's empty shack and made his way merrily back home, where he told his father and brothers a long tale of how during the night he had met a creature with bristling whiskers and bushy beard, cat-like face and saucer eyes who was actually Satan in disguise. He told them that as he was about to kill this creature it begged him for mercy, and he spared its life in return for a promise that their wheat would never be bothered again.

The brothers laughed and laughed at this tale until they could laugh no more and let Ivan sleep on the top of the stove.

Several days later, Danilo happened upon the shepherd's shack, where he saw two handsome steeds with manes of golden hair, and beside them in its stall stood a horse so queer and small with two humps on his little back, coal black eyes and ears a yard long!

Danilo was overcome with amazement at the sight of the three horses and ran all the way home to tell his brother Gavrilo. The two rushed back to the hut. They realized that Ivan must have hidden the horses there. When they reached the shack they saw:

Two chargers, snorting, ruby eyes ablaze,
Silken tails in ringlets streaming,
Golden in the shadows gleaming.
And their hoofs, of diamonds made,
Were with monster pearls inlaid.

The two brothers decided that these marvelous horses could be destined only for a Tsar to ride. So they decided to take them to the Fair, which took place opposite the Palace of the Tsar, where they could be sold.

When Ivan returned to the shepherd's hut, he found that his wondrous steeds were gone and only little Humpback remained. Ivan was overcome with sorrow at the loss of the two chargers, but Humpback bade him mount on his back and promised him that he would find whoever had stolen his horses.

Up on the pony's back strode Ivan, and they raced through the sky until they caught up with his brothers, who were leading the steeds. Ivan upbraided them for stealing his horses, and the brothers appealed to his mercy. He forgave them and the three stopped for the night, tying the steeds under a leafy tree.

In a little while they saw a bright light from afar. Danilo and Gavrilo had never seen such a light, and, being fearful of it, they told their youngest brother to go and fetch it. Ivan mounted little Humpback and rode off towards the bright light.

There the field was bright as day, lit by wondrous brilliant rays, cold and smokeless in their blaze. Ivan was speechless: so much light and no heat coming from it. What a curious light!

Little Humpback warned Ivan not to touch the light, for it was a Firebird's feather:

"Ivan, for your own sake,
Touch it not, for in its wake
Sorrows, many woes
Follow everywhere it goes."

But Ivan was consumed with curiosity and did not listen to Humpback. He took the feather and wrapped it in his hat, after which he galloped back to his brothers on the pony's back.

"Handsome horses, black as night . . ."

Fedoskino

The Tsar was overwhelmed by the steeds.

Palekh

When he returned to his brothers, he told them that the light had gone out when he had gotten to it.

The next day, they went to the Hostler's Fair opposite the Palace. As was the custom, nothing could be sold unless the Mayor gave his permission, and when the Mayor saw the wondrous chargers he immediately rushed to the Tsar to tell him about them, which was exactly what the brothers thought he would do. The Mayor described the horses to the Tsar:

> "Handsome horses, black as night,
> Silken manes in ringlets bright,
> Golden in the sunlight streaming,
> Flowing tails, all golden gleaming,
> And their hoofs, of diamonds made,
> Were with monster pearls inlaid."

The Tsar became so excited that he decided then and there that he had to have these horses for his own. He immediately drove to the Fair and was overwhelmed and charmed by the steeds. He paid Ivan what he asked for the steeds and more, and ordered his grooms to take them to the royal stables. However, the horses would not go with the grooms, so the Tsar issued a decree making Ivan Master of the Horses so that he could take care of the steeds, promising him that he would have everything he wanted: handsome raiment, plenty of food, the life of a lord.

Ivan agreed readily and went to the palace, where he lived in great luxury. However, the Royal Chamberlain was very jealous and tried mightily to find some way to make the Tsar angry with Ivan. One night he hid in the stables and saw Ivan take out the magic Firebird's feather, which gave off a light so bright that the Chamberlain almost swooned in fright.

The next morning the Chamberlain went to the Tsar and told him that Ivan not only had the Firebird's feather, but had boasted that he could have the Firebird itself if he wished. When the Tsar heard this, he bade Ivan be brought to him and instructed him under threat of death to bring the Firebird to him immediately!

Ivan returned to the stable, where he cried out his woes to little Humpback, who reminded him that he had told him not to take the feather nor even to touch it. Now, however, since the deed was done and Ivan needed his help, Humpback gave him the following instructions:

> "Say to the Tsar — I need the best of grain,
> And two troughs too, if you please.
> Wine, brought in from overseas.
> Tell them that they must make haste,
> For I have no time to waste.
> I'll be off at dawn of day."

The Tsar gave strict commands to fulfill Ivan's demands and sent him off with his blessings to find the Firebird.

On the eighth day of riding, little Humpback stopped at a glade, in back of which was a hill made of silver, and told Ivan that this was where the Firebirds flocked before dawn to drink water from the stream. He then instructed him to mix wine and grain in one trough and to hide himself from sight behind the second one, to make no sound and to keep his eyes and ears alert. At dawn, flocks of Firebirds came to the glade, and they ate the grain mixed with wine. Since they were drunk from the wine and unsteady on their feet, it was possible for Ivan to snare one of the Firebirds and put it in his sack.

21

When Ivan brought the Firebird back to the palace, the Tsar was so delighted that he made Ivan his Royal Groom, a position even higher than he had held before.

Now the Chamberlain was more jealous than ever and more firmly committed to finding some way to get rid of Ivan.

Some time later, the Chamberlain told the Tsar that Ivan had boasted that he knew the wondrous Tsar-Maid, that most beautiful of all beings, and could, if he wished, bring her to the Kingdom.

The Tsar again called Ivan and commanded him to bring the Tsar-Maid to the Palace.

Ivan rushed off to the hayloft where little Humpback lay and poured out his troubles:

"Oh, my Humpback dear,
   I must bring the Tsar-Maid here!
   Oh, whatever shall I do?"

Little Humpback told Ivan to stop his weeping for he would help him. However, it was necessary for Ivan to tell the Tsar the following:

"To catch the Tsar-Maid, Sire,
   Two large cloths I shall require,
   And a tent of gold brocade.
   And a dinner-service, made
   All of gold, from overseas;
   Sweetmeats, too, her taste to please."

Ivan did as Humpback bade him and received all these things from the Tsar, who blessed him and sped him on his way.

Ivan put the cloths and tent, dinner service and sweetmeats on the back of the pony and flew away to seek the Tsar-Maid. Seven days they rode, and on the eighth day they stood in a dark and dense green wood where Humpback stopped and said:

"See — the ocean lies ahead.
   There it is, the whole year round,
   This Tsar-Maiden can be found;
   Only twice a year, not more,
   Does she spend the day on shore.
   And, tomorrow, I've a notion,
   We shall see her on the ocean."

They galloped to the ocean shore where Ivan, upon directions from his pony, pitched the tent of gold brocade and laid the cloth, service of gold and the sweetmeats. Then he hid behind the tent.

It was early morn when the Tsar-Maid's ship came to the shore. She stood proudly at the prow, steering the boat towards the beach, with her *Gusli* slung over her shoulder. It was said that so sweet was her voice and so beautiful the music she played on her *Gusli*, no one could resist her.

The Tsar-Maid beached her boat and went into the brocade tent. Ivan, remembering the warnings that Humpback had given him that he was not to listen to her singing or else he would be enchanted, ran into the tent and seized her by her beautiful long tresses.

Holding her tight, he placed her behind him on Humpback, and they sped back to the palace of the Tsar.

When the Tsar saw the beautiful Maid, he begged her to marry him, but she spurned him and said that she would marry only the one who could bring her signet-ring to her from the bottom of the ocean.

The Tsar called Ivan to him and told him to find the Tsar-Maid's ring, so once more Ivan and his Pony left the palace on another adventure. As they left, the Tsar-Maid called out to him to be sure to visit her green mansions and to convey greetings to her mother, the Moon, and her brother, the Sun.

It was said that so sweet was the Tsar-Maid's voice, no one could resist her.

Kholui

22

Ivan and the Pony rode off. The horse flew like the wind, leaving miles and leagues behind. Twenty thousand leagues they traveled ere each night came. Near the sea, the pony neighed and told Ivan:

> "We will reach a glade in a minute, maybe more,
> Leading to the ocean shore,
> Where, with monster head and tail,
> Lies the Monster-Marvel Whale.
> These ten years he lies in pain,
> Ignorant of how to gain
> Pardon, to this very day.
> He will humbly beg and pray
> That you will pardon for him gain
> When we reach the Sun's domain.
> Promise him, Ivan, and see
> That you do so faithfully."

Sure enough, when they reached the sea, Ivan saw a monster whale with huge holes and sores in his hide. Vegetables and flowers grew out of these holes, children were playing on his back, people had built houses there, too. When the whale saw Ivan, he begged him to go to the Sun and ask for forgiveness for him. If he would do that, he, the whale, would be of great help to Ivan some day!

Ivan promised the whale that he would intercede for him with the Sun, and off he rode to the palace of the Tsar-Maid's mother, the Moon.

Up above the earth they flew, until far off in the East, high above the earth, gleaming in the dawn, was the palace of the Sun and Moon.

> "Palace portals met their sight,
> Crowned in crystal, gleaming bright;
> All its pillars made of gold,
> Twisted cunningly, and scrolled.
> On each pillar shone a star;
> Round the palace, near and far,
> Fragrant gardens, fair to see,
> Spread in verdant brilliancy.
> Birds of paradise were singing
> In their golden cages, swinging.
> 'Mong the silver branches
> Mansions rose there, tall and fair."

Through the portals of this wondrous place, Ivan and the Pony entered. There he saw the Moon and gave her greetings from her daughter, the Tsar-Maid. When the Moon found out that the old Tsar wished to marry her beautiful young daughter, she was furious. In the meantime, Ivan begged her to tell him why the whale had been so sorely punished by the Moon and the Sun. She explained that, years ago, he had swallowed thirty ships, crew and all. When Ivan interceded for the whale and asked Moon to stop his suffering, she promised him that she would see to it that the whale was reprieved.

Moon then told Ivan to tell her daughter the Tsar-Maid that she should cease grieving, for she would never be married to the old toothless Tsar. Moon would see to it that her daughter married a young and handsome man.

Ivan took his leave and rode away on Humpback. When he came to the ocean shore he told the whale that the only way out of his troubles was to give up the thirty ships he had swallowed so long ago, with their sails and sailors, boats and oars. With a mighty roar, the Monster Whale turned round and thrashed the ocean with his tail. Then a fleet of thirty ships, one by one, were cast out from his jaws — sails and sailors, boats and oars.

As if by magic all the sores and holes disappeared from his hide, and the Mighty Whale lifted up his voice and cried out to Ivan:

> "Tell me friend, what can I do
> In return, or give to you?
> Would you care for golden fish?
> Lovely pearls? Anything
> You may ask for, I will bring."

Off he rode to the palace of the Moon. *Palekh*

Ivan told the whale that he wanted nothing from him except the signet ring of the Tsar-Maid, which rested at the bottom of the sea. At this, the Monster Whale sent all the creatures of the sea to search for the ring. Two white sturgeons could not find the ring; a pair of dolphins searched to no avail. Neither carp nor herring, nor any other fish could find it. Finally, the sea creatures asked the perch if he had seen the ring. He had, and told them that it was in a small casket which weighed more than a ton. He asked all the fish to help him get the casket out from the bottom of the sea, and they gave it to the whale, who then brought it to Ivan, waiting at the sea shore.

Said the whale:

> "Now I've paid my debt, I'll go.
> But should you need me anew,
> Call me, and I'll come to you.
> I'll remember till I die
> What you've done for me — good-bye!"

23

Ivan could not lift the casket which contained the ring, but little Humpback raised the casket from the ground to his neck with one light kick and said:

"Now mount me, quick.
Time is nearly up, you know,
And we still have far to go."

Horse and rider reached the palace of the Tsar tired and worn. As soon as they arrived, the Tsar ran out to meet them.

"Where's the ring?" was all he said.

Ivan got off from his horse and proudly answered that the ring was in the little casket, but that it would take many guards to lift it. The guards came out and lifted the casket, and the Tsar took the ring from it and rushed off to give it to the Tsar-Maid.

But even though he had brought her the ring, the Tsar-Maid still refused to marry the Tsar.

"Only look — you're old and grey,
I'm but fifteen and a day.
We can't marry, if we do,
All the Tsars will laugh at you,
Saying: There goes youth with age.
Never, never in my life,
Will I ever be the wife
Of an old old man like you,
Grey haired, ugly, toothless, too!"

The Tsar was grief-stricken and asked the Maid what he could do, for certainly there was no way to regain his youth. Only God could work such wonders.

At this the Maid said that if he had no fear of pain, he could do the following to regain his youth: he must give orders that in the early morn there must be three cauldrons placed in the palace courtyard. Two were to have fires burning steadily under them. In one, there was to be water boiling; in the second, milk must be heated until it boiled. The third cauldron was to contain chilled water.

The Maid continued that if the Tsar wished to become young and handsome again and to marry her, he must first divest himself of all his robes, plunge into the milk, next into the boiling water, and then into the cold water. When he emerged from the third cauldron, he would be young again!

After hearing this, the old Tsar called Ivan and told him that on the morrow he would find three cauldrons in the courtyard that he was to test for the Tsar. He must first divest himself of his clothes, bathe in the milk, then in the boiling water, and then in the cold water.

Never had anyone seen a grander Prince.

24

Palekh

Ivan, frightened, crept back to the hayloft where he told his sad tale to little Humpback. The little pony told Ivan not to worry and instructed him as follows:

"Listen, lad, tomorrow morn,
When you strip there on the lawn,
Say: 'Your Gracious Majesty!
Please to send my horse to me
So that I can say good-bye
To my horse before I die.'
Now, I know he will agree,
And he'll send a groom for me.
I will wave my tail about,
In each cauldron, dip my snout,
Then I'll squirt upon you, twice,
Whistle long and loudly thrice.
You — be sure to look alive,
In the milk then quickly dive,
Dive, just as you have been told.
Now, my lad, go, say your prayers,
Sleep in peace, forget your cares."

So Ivan did as he was told, and when dawn arrived he went to the courtyard, where the fires were already burning steadily under the two cauldrons. All the people of the court were there to watch the proceedings.

Ivan did exactly as he had been told. The pony was brought to him and Ivan dove into the milk, then the boiling water and then the chilled water.

When he emerged, he was so handsome that no words could describe him. He dried himself and dressed, bowed low to the Tsar-Maid and glanced around with a princely air. Never had anyone seen a grander prince.

Seeing this, the Tsar hastily undressed, crossed his breast twice and thrice, and dived into the first cauldron, whereupon he was boiled to death on the spot!

Then the Tsar-Maid stood up and raised her hand for silence. Unveiling her face, which was the fairest that any eye had ever seen, she addressed the populace:

"Listen, now! The Tsar is dead.
Will you have me in his stead?
Am I pleasing in your eyes?
Speak! If so, then recognise
As the Lord of all the land,
My beloved husband."

And pointing to Ivan, she placed her fair arm around his waist.

All the populace shouted that they were willing to make her their Tsarina and Ivan their Tsar.

Ivan and the Tsar-Maid were married with great pomp and festivities and lived happily ever after.

The Humpbacked pony was never seen again.

Ivan rides to the palace of the Moon and the Sun. Below are the Tsar-Maid and the Monster Whale.   *Palekh*

Vasilisa the Beautiful

He was dressed in red, his horse was red, and the horse's harness was red too. (Shown actual size)

Palekh

Long, long ago, in a faraway Tsardom, there lived an old man and an old woman and their lovely daughter, Vasilisa. Although their hut was small and they were not rich, they lived a happy and peaceful life.

But even the brightest of skies may become overcast, and misfortune struck this happy household when the old woman fell gravely ill. Feeling that her end was near, she called Vasilisa to her bedside, embraced her, and gave her a little doll, saying:

"My dear child, do as I tell you. Take good care of this little doll and never show it to anyone. If ever anything bad happens to you, give the doll something to eat and ask its advice. She will help you out of all your troubles."

She gave Vasilisa a last kiss and embrace, and died.

The old man sorrowed and grieved for his wife for a long time, but finally married again, for he wanted to give his beloved daughter a second mother. But unfortunately he married a woman who was a cruel stepmother to his child.

The stepmother had two daughters of her own. They were mean and spiteful, but their mother loved them dearly and was always kissing and hugging them. However, she never let Vasilisa have a moment's peace. She was constantly nagging and scolding her. Vasilisa was very unhappy because her stepmother and stepsisters made her do all the work in the house. She had to mix the dough, make the fire, sweep the floors, milk the cow, fetch the wood — all the menial tasks which they themselves did not like to do.

Vasilisa did all that she was told to do and always got her chores done on time. And instead of becoming ugly and worn from all the work, as the stepmother and stepsisters had planned, each day Vasilisa became more beautiful. Of course, they did not know about the little doll that helped Vasilisa with everything.

Every morning Vasilisa would milk the cow and then lock herself in the pantry. She would give some milk to the doll and say, "Come, little doll, drink your milk, my dear, and I'll pour out all my troubles in your little ear."

And the doll would drink the milk and comfort Vasilisa and do all her work for her. Vasilisa would sit in the shade, twining flowers into her long braid, and before she knew it the vegetable gardens were weeded, the fire lighted, the water brought in, the floors scrubbed, and all the chores done. The doll even showed her an herb which Vasilisa could use against sun-burn so that her skin remained milk-white and fair, and as she used the herb she became even more beautiful. Such was her beauty as could not be pictured and could not be told, but was a true wonder and joy to behold.

One day the old man had to leave his family to go on a long journey, leaving them all alone in the house. The hut stood at the edge of a deep and dense forest where Baba-Yaga, the cunning and sly witch lived. It was said that Baba-Yaga gobbled people up in a matter of a second.

One dark evening, the stepmother gave some work to each of the sisters. The first was to weave lace, the second was to knit stockings, and Vasilisa was to spin yarn. The stepmother then put out all the lights in the house, except for a single piece of birch wood which burned in one corner where the sisters were working, and went to bed.

The birch wood snapped and crackled for a short time and then went out.

"What are we to do?" cried the stepsisters. "It is dark but we must work. One of us will have to go to Baba-Yaga's house and ask for a light."

The elder sister said that she would not go because she could see by the light of her needle.

The second sister said she would not go because she could knit by the light of her knitting needles.

Then both of them said, as one, "Vasilisa is the one, she must go for the light! Go to Baba-Yaga's house immediately." And with this they pushed her out of the house and closed the door tightly behind her.

Vasilisa burst into tears. It was dark and the wind blew, and she was very frightened. She took out her little doll and spoke to it. "Oh my dear little doll, what am I to do? Baba-Yaga gobbles people up, bones and all. I am so frightened!"

"Do not be frightened, Vasilisa," the doll whispered. "No harm will come to you while I am with you."

Vasilisa thanked the doll and set off for Baba-Yaga's house.

She walked and walked, trembling with fear, holding the little doll close to her. Suddenly she saw a man on horseback galloping past. He was dressed all in white, his horse was white and the horse's harness, which was silver, gleamed white in the darkness.

It was almost dawn now, and Vasilisa walked on, stumbling and stubbing her toes against tree roots and stumps. Drops of dew glistened on her beautiful long braid. Suddenly another horseman came galloping by. He was dressed in red, his horse was red and the horse's harness was red, too.

The sun rose, kissed Vasilisa and warmed her and dried the dew on her hair. Vasilisa walked for a whole day, and it was almost evening when she came to a small clearing. She saw a hut standing there. The fence around the hut was made of human bones and crowned with human skulls. The gate was made of the bones of men's legs, the bolts were the bones of men's arms, and the lock was a set of sharp teeth.

Vasilisa stopped in horror at the sight. Suddenly a horseman came riding up. He was dressed in black, his horse was black and the horse's harness was also black. The horseman galloped up to the gate and vanished in the air.

As night descended, lo and behold! the eyes of the skulls crowning the fence began to glow, and the light from these eyes was so bright it became as light as though it were day.

She walked and walked
in the forest . . .
holding the little doll
close to her.

28

Palekh

There was Baba Yaga flying up in a mortar, sweeping away her tracks with a broom.

Palekh

Vasilisa shook with fear; she could not move. Suddenly, the earth trembled and rocked beneath her, and there was Baba-Yaga flying up in a mortar, swinging her pestle like a whip and sweeping the tracks away with a broom. She flew up to the gate and, sniffing the air, cried, "I smell Russian flesh! Who is here?"

Vasilisa bowed low to Baba-Yaga and said very humbly, "It is I, Vasilisa. My stepsisters sent me to you to ask for a light."

"Oh, it's you, is it?" Baba-Yaga replied. "Your stepmother is a relation of mine. So, stay with me for a short while and work, and we'll see what is to be seen."

Baba-Yaga ordered the gates to open and rode in on her mortar, with Vasilisa following. There was a birch-tree at the gate which started to lash out at Vasilisa with its branches. Baba-Yaga ordered it to stop. When they came to the house, a dog lay at the door and started to growl at Vasilisa and was about to bite her. Baba-Yaga ordered it to stop. They came inside, and in the passageway there was an old mean cat who made moves to scratch Vasilisa with its sharp claws. Baba-Yaga ordered it to leave her alone.

She turned to Vasilisa and said, "You see, my pretty one, it will not be easy for you to run away from me. My cat will scratch you, my dog will bite you, my birch-tree will lash you and put out your eyes, and my gate will not open to let you out. So do not try to run away."

Saying this, Baba-Yaga went to her room and stretched out on a bench, ordering her maid to make her a meal.

"Come, black-browed maid, give us something to eat," she cried.

And the black-browed maid brought her a huge pot of borscht and half a cow, ten jugs of milk and a roasted sow, twenty chickens and forty geese, two whole pies and an extra piece, cider and meat and home-brewed ale, beer by the barrel and kvass by the pail.

Baba-Yaga ate everything up and drank everything down, but she gave Vasilisa only a piece of bread for her supper.

"Now, Vasilisa," she said, "take this big sack of millet and pick it over seed by seed. And if it is not perfectly clean, I shall eat you up!"

With this, Baba-Yaga closed her eyes, went to sleep and began to snore as loud as thunder.

Vasilisa did not eat the bread, but put it before her little doll and told her all her troubles. The doll comforted her and said, "Do not grieve and do not weep, but close your eyes and go to sleep. For morning is wiser than evening."

As soon as Vasilisa slept, the doll called out to all the birds to come and help in the work. The birds came flying from all sides, flocks and flocks of them, more than the eye could see or tongue could tell. They began to pick over the millet seed by seed very quickly indeed. They placed the good seeds into the sack and threw the bad seeds away. Before the night was over the sack was filled to the top with clean seeds. They finished just as the white horseman galloped past the gate on his white horse. Day was dawning. Baba-Yaga awoke and was furious to find that the task which she had set for Vasilisa was finished, but there was nothing to be done. So she huffed and grumbled and then told Vasilisa to take a sack which stood in a corner filled with peas and poppy seeds and to separate the peas from the seeds and put them in two separate heaps. If the task was not done by the time she returned, she would eat Vasilisa!

29

Baba-Yaga went out into the yard and whistled, and the mortar and pestle came up to her. The red horseman galloped past, and the sun rose. Baba-Yaga climbed into the mortar and rode out of the yard, swinging her pestle like a whip and whisking away her tracks with a broom.

After she left, Vasilisa took a crust of bread, fed her little doll and wept bitterly. The doll comforted her and told her not to worry. She called the mice from the house, the barn and the fields to come and help in the work that had to be done. And the mice came running — more than the eye could see or the tongue could tell. Within the hour the work was all done.

It was getting on toward evening, and the black-browed maid set the table and began to wait for Baba-Yaga's return.

The black horseman galloped past the gate, night fell, and the eyes of the skulls crowning the fence began to glow. The trees groaned and crackled, the leaves rustled, and Baba-Yaga came riding home in her mortar.

When the witch found out that Vasilisa had done everything she had instructed her to do during the day, she was very frustrated, but said nothing. She told Vasilisa to go to bed, saying that she too would go to sleep in a short while. Vasilisa went behind the stove, and she heard Baba-Yaga say to her maid:

"Light the stove, and make the fire hot. When I wake up, I shall roast Vasilisa!"

Baba-Yaga lay down on a bench, placed her chin on a shelf, covered herself with her foot and began to snore so loudly that the whole forest trembled and shook.

Vasilisa burst into piteous tears, took a crust of bread and put it before her doll. The doll told her exactly what to do.

Vasilisa rushed to the black-browed maid and bowed low to her.

"Please, dear maiden, help me!" she cried. "When you light the stove, pour water over the wood so it does not burn the way it should. Take my silk kerchief to reward you for your good deed."

The maid told Vasilisa that she would help her. She would take a long time to heat the stove and she would tickle Baba-Yaga's heels and scratch them too so that she would sleep very soundly the whole night through. And then she told Vasilisa to run away.

"But won't the three horsemen catch me and bring me back?" asked Vasilisa.

The black-browed maid answered, "Oh no, the white horseman is the bright day, the red horseman is the golden sun, and the black horseman is the black night. They will not touch you."

Vasilisa thanked the maid and ran out into the passage. The cat rushed at her and was about to scratch her, but she threw him a small pie and he did not touch her.

She ran from the porch, and the dog ran out and was about to bite her, but she threw him a piece of bread, and the dog let her go. She ran out to the yard, and the birch-tree tried to lash her. But she tied the tree with a ribbon, and it let her pass. The gate was about to shut before her, but Vasilisa greased its hinges and it swung open.

Vasilisa ran into the dark forest, and just then the black horseman galloped by and it became pitch black all around. She was terrified and asked the little doll what to do. Following the doll's advice, she took one of the skulls from the fence and, mounting it on a stick, set off across the forest. Its eyes glowed, and by their light the dark night was as bright as day.

(Shown actual size)

She took one of the skulls from the fence and mounted it on a stick.   Palekh

30

When Baba-Yaga awoke, she saw that Vasilisa had run away. She rushed out to ask her cat, her dog, her tree and her gate if they had allowed Vasilisa to leave. They all told her that they had, for Vasilisa had been kinder to them in one day than the witch had been in the years they had served her faithfully.

When Vasilisa arrived home, she found that there was no light in the house. Her stepsisters told her that since she had left they had not been able to keep a light on in the house. They had tried everything, and even when neighbors had brought in light, the moment it was brought into their house, it would immediately go out.

Seeing the glowing skull which Vasilisa was carrying, they took it away from her and brought it into the house, saying that perhaps at last this light would keep burning.

When the skull was brought into the house, the eyes fixed themselves on the stepmother and her two daughters and burned them like fire. They tried to hide, but run where they would, the eyes followed them and never let them out of their sight. By morning, the stepmother and her daughters were burned to a cinder, and only Vasilisa remained unharmed.

She buried the skull outside the hut, and a bush of red roses grew up on the spot.

After this, Vasilisa, not wanting to stay in the hut in the forest by herself, went into the village and made her home in the house of an old woman, who was very kind to her.

One day Vasilisa asked the old woman to buy some fine flax, the best that could be found, for she was bored doing nothing and wanted to weave.

The old woman bought the flax, and Vasilisa began to spin yarn. She worked quickly. The spinning wheel hummed along and the golden thread came out so thin and so even as had never been seen before. When she was through spinning, she began to weave cloth, and it turned out so fine that it could be passed through the eye of a needle, like a thread. She bleached the cloth, and it came out whiter than snow.

Vasilisa gave the cloth to the old woman and told her to sell it and keep the money to repay her for her kindness. When the woman saw the magnificent cloth, she told Vasilisa that such cloth was only fit for a Tsarevich to wear.

The old woman took the cloth to the palace, and when the Tsarevich saw it he was filled with wonder. He asked the old woman how much she wanted for the cloth, but she replied that it was not for sale, but was a present for him. The Tsarevich thanked the old woman, showered her with gifts and sent her home. But he could not find anyone to make a shirt of the cloth for him, since it was so fine that no one could work on it. So he sent for the old woman and said:

"You wove this fine cloth, so you must know how to make a shirt out of it."

The Red Knight passes Baba Yaga's hut.   Palekh

The old woman replied that it was not she who had spun the yarn or woven the cloth, but a beautiful maid named Vasilisa.

The Tsarevich then bade the old woman ask Vasilisa to make the shirts for him. The old woman went home and told Vasilisa what had transpired.

Vasilisa made two shirts from the cloth, embroidered them with silken threads, studded them with large round pearls and gave them to the old woman to take to the palace. She then sat down at the window with a piece of embroidery.

By and by, servants of the Tsar came to bid Vasilisa to come to the palace.

Vasilisa went to the palace, and when the Tsarevich saw her he was smitten with her incomparable beauty.

"I shall never let you leave me," said the Tsarevich. "You shall be my bride this very day."

He took both her lovely hands in his and placed her in the seat beside his own.

And so Vasilisa the Beautiful and the Tsarevich were married, and when Vasilisa's father returned soon afterwards, he lived in the palace with them. Vasilisa brought the kind old woman to live in the palace, too.

As for the little doll, Vasilisa carried it close to her forever.

The Tale of the Firebird, Tsarevich Ivan and the Gray Wolf

Tsarevich Ivan, the Firebird, Gray Wolf and the Fair Elena.   Palekh

Once upon a time, there lived a mighty Tsar. He had three sons. The oldest was Tsarevich Dimitri, the second was Tsarevich Vasily and the third was Tsarevich Ivan.

The mighty Tsar had a magnificent palace and a garden so beautiful that there was none finer anywhere on this earth. All kinds of beautiful flowers, trees and shrubs grew in his garden, but the Tsar's favorite was an apple tree which bore golden apples.

Time went on, and the Tsar noticed that many of his apples were being picked during the nights. He found out that every night, while the court slept, the Firebird flew into his garden and picked as many apples as she wished.

He called his sons to him and told them, "My beloved sons, the Firebird has been stealing my golden apples. Which one of you can catch her? If one of you captures her alive, I will give him half my kingdom while I live and the rest of it upon my death."

His sons answered as one, "We will try to capture the Firebird for you."

The first night, the eldest son went into the garden to keep watch. He sat near the apple tree, and as the night wore on he became very drowsy and fell asleep. While he slept, the Firebird flew into the garden, picked some apples, and flew away.

In the morning, the Tsar asked Dimitri if he had seen the Firebird. He answered that she had not come into the garden that night.

The first ballet for which Igor Stravinsky wrote a score was based on this fairy tale. It was commissioned by Diaghilev and choreographed by Fokine.

The next night, Vasily went to keep watch in the garden. He also sat under the apple tree, and in several hours, he too fell asleep. While he slept, the Firebird flew into the garden, picked many apples, and flew away. The next morning the Tsar asked whether he had seen the Firebird, and Vasily answered that she had not come into the garden that night.

The third night, it was Tsarevich Ivan's turn to keep watch in the garden, and he sat under the apple tree. For several hours, nothing happened. Then, suddenly, the whole garden was illuminated by a radiant golden light. The Firebird flew in. Her eyes sparkled like huge crystals; her wings were golden flames. She perched on the tree and began to pick the apples. Tsarevich Ivan stole up to her softly and tried to catch her. Although he could not hold her, he was able to seize her tail, and as the Firebird tore herself from his grasp, one beautiful luminous feather remained in Ivan's hand.

In the morning Ivan went to his father and gave him the feather of the Firebird. The Tsar was very pleased that his youngest son had finally succeeded in getting at least one feather from the Firebird. He took the feather into his chamber. When it was brought in, the entire room glowed as though it was lit by thousands of candles.

From that time on, the Firebird did not come into the garden, but the Tsar was obsessed with the idea that he had to have her in his palace.

The Firebird tore herself from his grasp.
(Shown actual size)

Palekh

33

. . . one beautiful luminous feather remained in Ivan's hand.

He summoned his three sons to him and bade them go out and find the Firebird for him.

The two eldest sons were filled with envy that their younger brother had succeeded in obtaining the Firebird's feather when they had failed completely, so they set out together on their quest, after obtaining their father's blessings. The Tsar tried to keep his youngest son in the palace while the two older brothers were gone, but he could not pursuade Ivan to stay. So after he too obtained the Tsar blessing, Ivan chose a horse and rode out from the palace.

Whether he rode for a long time or a little, or whether the distance was a short one or a long one, no one could tell, but he rode until he came to a large open field. In the middle of this field was a tall pillar, and on the pillar were written the following words:

"Whoever goes from this spot on the road straight before him will be hungry and cold. Whoever goes from this spot to the right will be safe, but his horse will be killed. Whoever goes from this spot to the left will be killed himself, but his horse will be safe."

Tsarevich Ivan read the inscriptions and went to the right, thinking that even though his horse might be killed, he himself would be safe and could find another horse.

He rode for three days when suddenly out of nowhere a great gray wolf came toward him and asked him why he had come in this direction when he knew that his horse would be killed. And saying this, he devoured the horse and ran away.

Ivan wept for his horse, and then continued his journey on foot. He walked and walked until he was exhausted. He was about to sit down and rest when the gray wolf appeared again. He told Ivan that he felt sorry for him and was also very sorry that he had eaten his horse. To make up for his horrible deed, he told Ivan to get up on his back, and he would take him wherever he wished to go.

Ivan told the gray wolf the purpose of his journey. Hearing this, the wolf ran much faster than any horse.

When night fell, they came to a stone wall. There the wolf stopped and told Ivan to climb over the stone wall into the garden, where he would find the Firebird in a golden cage. He instructed Ivan to take the Firebird, but to be sure not to take the golden cage, for if he touched the cage he would be caught.

Ivan climbed into the garden where all was still as death. He took the Firebird out of the cage, but before he left the garden, he thought to himself that he was very foolish to leave the magnificent golden cage for, indeed, where would he put the Firebird? So he went back for the cage, and the moment he touched it, there was a great hue and cry, the guards awoke and caught Ivan with the Firebird. They immediately led him to their Tsar, Dolmat.

The Tsar was furious with Ivan and berated him for trying to steal the Firebird from his garden.

"Who are you, and where do you come from?" he asked.

Ivan answered that he was the son of Tsar Vyslav and explained that the Firebird had stolen his father's golden apples nightly, which was the reason he had come to take it away.

The Tsar answered that if Tsarevich Ivan had come to him and told him the whole story, he would have given him the Firebird. But since he had come under the cover of night and tried to steal it, he had disgraced himself and his family. However, the Tsar offered to give him the Firebird if Tsarevich Ivan would go to the Thirtieth Kingdom beyond Twenty Nine Lands and obtain for him the horse with the golden mane from the Kingdom of Tsar Afron. But if he failed, Dolmat would proclaim in all the Tsardoms that Ivan was a thief.

Ivan went to the gray wolf and told him everything. The wolf berated him for not listening to him and trying to take the cage in spite of the fact that he had warned him against doing just that. However, he finally relented and told Ivan to sit on his back. He would take him to the horse with the golden mane!

Ivan got on the back of the gray wolf, who took off

34

as fast as lightning. The wolf ran until night fell, and they arrived at the royal stables of Tsar Afron. There the gray wolf told Tsarevich Ivan to go into the stables and take the horse with the golden mane, but not to dare to touch the golden bridle which hung on the wall beside him.

Ivan entered the stables, took the horse and began to leave, but when he noticed the magnificent golden bridle on the wall he could not resist taking it. No sooner had he done so than there was a furious noise. The stable boys woke up at once, caught him, and brought him to Tsar Afron, who questioned him, just as Dolmat had done.

Tsar Afron, as had Dolmat before him, told Ivan that if he had come to him and told him beforehand what he wanted, he would have given him the horse with the golden mane. However, since he had come stealthily, under cover of night, he would proclaim his dishonor in all the Tsardoms. But he would give Ivan a way out. If he would go beyond the Thrice Ninth Land, to the Thrice Tenth Kingdom and bring back to him the beautiful Princess, Elena the Fair, he would be forgiven his offense. Tsar Afron loved Elena dearly, but could not win her as his bride.

So Ivan again came to the gray wolf and told him everything that had happened. Again the wolf berated him for not listening to him, but still he agreed to take him where he had to go.

Prince Ivan mounted the gray wolf's back, and the wolf ran fast as an arrow, as can happen in fairy tales. In a very short time, he arrived in the Kingdom of Elena the Fair. Reaching the golden fence that surrounded her palace and garden, the wolf told Ivan to go back along the same road that they had come on and to sit under the green oak tree they had passed and wait for him.

Ivan went where he was told. The gray wolf sat near the golden fence and waited there until Princess Elena took her walk in the garden with her ladies in waiting. When she entered the garden, the gray wolf quickly jumped over the fence, caught the Princess and ran to the place where Ivan was waiting.

Tsarevich Ivan seated himself beside the Princess on the back of the gray wolf, who then darted away toward Tsar Afron's kingdom. No matter how fast the Princess's guards pursued the gray wolf, they could not catch him.

During the long ride, as they sat together on the back of the gray wolf, Ivan and the Princess fell madly in love. But when they arrived at King Afron's kingdom, Ivan knew that, in spite of the fact that he loved the Princess dearly, he would have to lead her to the palace and give her to the Tsar. At that he grew exceedingly sad and wept bitterly. He told the wolf of his love for the Princess and begged him to help him once again. The wolf agreed to help him and told Ivan his plan: he would transform himself into the beautiful Princess, after which Ivan was to take him, in the guise of Elena, to Tsar Afron, who would give him the horse with the golden mane, for the Tsar would think that the wolf was indeed Princess Elena. Later, when Ivan had ridden far away on the horse with the golden mane, the wolf would ask the Tsar to let him walk in the open field, from which he could escape.

Ivan told the real Princess Elena to wait for him outside the town. The wolf transformed himself into the Princess and Ivan took him to the Tsar.

Afron was delighted when he saw the Princess and gave the horse with the golden mane to Tsarevich Ivan, who immediately mounted him and galloped away, picking up Elena at the appointed place. They rode off towards the kingdom of Tsar Dolmat. In the meantime, the gray wolf, in the guise of the beautiful Elena, lived with Tsar Afron one day and then begged to be allowed to walk in the open fields. Tsar Afron, so in love with Elena that he could deny her nothing, granted this wish to his beloved. As soon as the wolf got to the open field, he immediately escaped the kingdom.

Tsarevich Ivan rode with Elena next to him and was so taken with the beautiful Princess that he completely forgot about the gray wolf. Suddenly, seemingly from nowhere, the gray wolf appeared and told Ivan to ride on his back and let the Princess ride on the horse with the golden mane.

As they approached Tsar Dolmat's kingdom, Ivan begged the gray wolf to transform himself into the horse with the golden mane so that he himself could keep the real horse. The wolf agreed and changed himself into the golden-maned horse, upon which Tsarevich Ivan rode into the palace grounds of Tsar Dolmat, leaving Elena in the green meadow to await his return.

Tsar Dolmat was overjoyed to see the beautiful horse; he wined and feasted Tsarevich Ivan and, after two days of great celebration, gave the Firebird in the golden cage to Tsarevich Ivan, as he had promised.

Tsarevich Ivan took the Firebird, went to the outskirts of the town, mounted the horse with the golden mane together with Princess Elena the Fair and set out for his homeland.

Back in the kingdom of Dolmat, the Tsar decided on the next day to ride on his golden-maned horse in the open field. When he mounted him and tried to spur him on, it threw him and turned back into the gray wolf.

The gray wolf overtook Tsarevich Ivan and told him to mount him and let the Princess ride on the horse with the golden mane.

And so they continued on their journey. When the gray wolf brought them to the spot where first they had met he told Ivan, "Climb down from my back. This is the spot where I tore your horse in half, and this is the spot where I have brought you back safely. Now you have the horse with the golden mane; mount him, and go where you have to go. I am no longer your servant." And after speaking thus, the gray wolf ran off and Tsarevich Ivan set out on his way with his beautiful Elena.

He rode with her until they were close to his own land. They were so tired now that he stopped. They dismounted and lay down to rest under a tree. He tied the horse to the same tree and put the cage with the Firebird by his side. The two lovers spoke tenderly to each other and fell asleep.

While they were sleeping Tsarevich Ivan's brothers Dimitri and Vasily passed that way, returning empty handed from their own journeys. Seeing the horse and the Firebird in the cage near their sleeping brother and his Princess, they decided to kill him and take the prizes for their own. Dimitri drew his sword and stabbed Tsarevich Ivan and cut him into small pieces. He then awakened Elena, who realized that Ivan was dead. She was terribly frightened and began to weep bitterly.

Dimitri put the sword to Elena's heart and commanded her to tell the Tsar that it was they who had captured the horse and the Firebird, or else they would kill her as well as Ivan.

She was so frightened that she promised to do as they bade, and they took off for the palace of Tsar Vyslav.

Tsarevich Ivan lay dead for thirty days. Then the gray wolf came upon him and wanted to revive him but could not. At that moment the gray wolf saw a raven and her two young start to swoop down to eat the Tsarevich's body. The wolf hid behind a bush, and just as one of the young ravens started to eat Ivan, the wolf came out from behind the bush, grabbed the young raven and threatened to tear him in half. The mother of the raven flew to the ground and said to the wolf, "Oh gray wolf, do not touch my young child, he has done nothing to you!"

The gray wolf told the mother raven that he would not touch her child if she would fly beyond the Thrice Ninth land, to the Thrice Tenth Kingdom, and bring the water of death and the water of life to him. This the raven promised, and on the third day, she returned with two phials of water and gave them to the wolf.

The gray wolf sprinkled the water of death on the body of Tsarevich Ivan and immediately all the pieces of his body grew together. He then sprinkled him with the water of life, and the Tsarevich stood up.

"I have slept for a long time," he said.

"Yes," answered the wolf, "you would have slept forever if I had not brought you back to life!"

He then told Ivan how his brothers had slain him and taken the Princess Elena, the horse, and the Firebird. The gray wolf bade Tsarevich Ivan hurry back to his homeland, for Vasily was that very day to marry the fair Elena.

Tsarevich Ivan rode back to his father's palace, and found that the wedding had already taken place and that the guests were just starting in on the wedding feast. When Tsarevich Ivan entered the feasting chamber, the Fair Elena saw him, sprang up from the table and kissed him, crying out to everyone, "It is Prince Ivan who is my beloved bridgroom, not Vasily!"

When Tsar Vyslav asked her what was meant by this extraordinary turn of events, Elena told him how the brothers had threatened her with death if she told him the truth, how they had killed Tsarevich Ivan and stolen the golden-maned horse and the Firebird. At this, Tsar Vyslav became extremely angry and had Vasily and Dimitri thrown into the lowest dungeons of the palace.

Tsarevich Ivan married Elena the Fair, and they lived happily ever after.

Tsarevich Ivan and the Firebird.   Palekh
(Shown actual size)

Rusalka

Rusalka rises up from the water . . .
(Shown actual size)

Palekh

The libretto for the opera *Rusalka* by Antonin Dvořák is based on a poem by Pushkin.

Rusalka, a water nymph, is the favorite daughter of the Spirit of the Lake. She is disconsolate because she has fallen in love with a handsome young Prince and wants to become human so that she can know the warmth and tenderness of human love.

She confesses her desires to her father, who is saddened by her request, since he knows that it will bring her unhappiness. When he sees that she is adamant, he advises her to visit the old witch Jezibaba and ask for her help.

When Rusalka goes to Jezibaba for help, she grants her wish and gives her human form, but there are two conditions: she will not be able to speak to her Prince, and if he proves unfaithful to her, both will be forever damned!

Rusalka agrees to the conditions, and when she goes back to the shores of the lake, she encounters her Prince, who has been mysteriously and magnetically attracted there. The Prince is completely enchanted at the sight of her beauty. They fall into each other's arms, and the enraptured Prince takes Rusalka to his palace.

The palace is full of guests who have come there for the wedding of Rusalka and the Prince. In the time which has passed since he brought her to his home, the Prince is concerned and upset because Rusalka has not spoken to him, and he has begun to tire of her silent beauty. His eyes stray to a foreign Princess, who has come to the palace for the wedding.

At the Wedding Ball, the Spirit of the Lake emerges from the fountain and expresses his despair at what has happened to his beloved daughter. Rusalka runs to him and tells him of her misery at seeing the Prince paying warm attention to the foreign Princess at the Ball. They see the Prince and Princess embrace ardently in the shadows of the garden. Rusalka throws herself into her bridegroom's arms, and the Spirit of the Lake tells the Prince that he will never be free of Rusalka.

Since one of the conditions of the witch's granting of human form to Rusalka is that they would both be doomed if the Prince were unfaithful to her, Rusalka is now condemned to wander as a shadow for all time. She longs for death, but Jezibaba tells her that now only the shedding of human blood can redeem her from the curse which is hers to bear.

The Prince comes to the lake where first he saw Rusalka and calls to her to come back to him. He begs her forgiveness for his cruelty to her. She rises up from the water and tenderly explains to him why she had not been able to speak to him and give him the passionate assurances of her love that he wanted. She explains that now he would die at her caress.

Even though the Spirit of the Lake proclaims that Rusalka's fate will not be changed by her husband's sacrifice, the Prince begs for the kiss that he knows will cause his death.

They fall passionately into each other's arms and share the final tender glory of their love.

General Toptiggin

The strolling player, with Mishka at his side, begs a ride from a passing toika driver.   Palekh
(Shown actual size)

This is a poem about a strolling player and his bear Mishka. He begs a ride from a passing troika driver and after riding for some time they go into a tavern for a drink, leaving the bear in the troika. The patient horses wait for hours. Occasionally, Mishka clanks his chains.

> Darkness falls. The horses quake.
> Icy fetters bind them.
> Fiercer grows the bitter frost,
> Mishka stirs behind them.
> They are startled — make a plunge,
> Here begins the evil:
> Mishka gave a roar, and they
> Bolted straight as though the sleigh
> Had contained the devil.

In the dark the bear is thought to be a general, riding his sleigh rough-shod over the terrified peasants.

39

The Frog Princess

Tsarevich Ivan shot his arrow in the air.

Mstera

*Choosing the bride.
(Shown actual size)*

Mstera

Once upon a time, in a faraway kingdom, there lived a Tsar who had three sons. When his sons grew to manhood, the Tsar called them to him and told them that while he was still alive he would like to see them married and to rejoice at the sight of their children, his grandchildren.

The sons replied that if that was his wish, he was to tell them also whom he would like them to marry.

The Tsar instructed them to take their bows and arrows and go out into the open field. There each was to put on a blindfold and shoot an arrow into the sky, and wherever the arrow fell, they would find their bride.

40

The sons bowed low to their father and hurried out to the open field to follow his instructions.

The eldest son's arrow fell in a boyar's courtyard and was picked up by the boyar's daughter. The middle son's arrow fell in a rich merchant's yard and was picked up by the merchant's daughter. As for the youngest son, Tsarevich Ivan, his arrow shot up and flew away he knew not where. He went in search of it and walked and walked until he reached a marsh. To his amazement, there was a frog holding the arrow in its mouth. The Tsarevich said to the frog, "Frog, Frog, give me back my arrow."

The frog replied, "I will if you marry me!"

"What do you mean?" asked Ivan. "How can I marry a frog?"

"You must," replied the frog. "I am your destined bride."

The frog turned into beautiful Vasilisa.   Fedoskino

"What do you mean?" asked Ivan.   Fedoskino
"How can I marry a frog?"

Tsarevich Ivan was sad and crestfallen. But there was nothing to be done, so he picked up the frog and carried it home.

Three weddings were then celebrated. The eldest son was married to the boyar's daughter, the middle son to the merchant's daughter, and poor Ivan to the frog.

Some time passed, and the Tsar called his sons to his side and told them that he wanted each of their wives to sew a shirt for him so that he could see which was the best needle-woman.

The sons bowed low to their father and left him. The two eldest sons told their wives about their father's request, and they immediately started to sew. Tsarevich Ivan came home, sat down and hung his head. The frog hopped over the floor and up to him and asked him why he was so unhappy. Ivan told her about his father's request, and the frog said, "Do not grieve, Ivan, but go to bed, for morning is wiser than evening."

Tsarevich Ivan went to bed, and the frog hopped out to the porch, cast off its frog skin and turned into Vasilisa the Wise and Clever, a maiden more beautiful than any eye had seen or tongue could tell. She clapped her hands and cried out, "Come, my women and maids, make haste and set to work! Make me a shirt by tomorrow morning, like those my own father used to wear."

In the morning, Tsarevich Ivan awoke, and there was the frog hopping on the floor again, but the shirt was all ready and lying on the table wrapped in a handsome embroidered towel. Ivan was overjoyed. He took the shirt and went to his father, who was already busy receiving his two other sons' gifts. The eldest son laid out his wife's shirt, and the Tsar said that it would do only for a poor peasant to wear. The middle son laid out his wife's shirt, and the Tsar said that that one could be used only to go to the baths.

Then Tsarevich Ivan laid out his shirt, all beautifully embroidered in gold and silver, and the Tsar took one look at it and said, "Now that is a shirt to wear on holidays!" and embraced his youngest son.

The two elder sons went home and spoke with their wives, and they came to the conclusion that they had been wrong to laugh at Ivan's wife. They decided that she was no frog at all, but actually a witch.

Some time later, the Tsar again called his sons together and bade them have their wives bake bread by the next morning, since he wanted to know which of them was the best cook.

Again Ivan went to the frog, and when she asked him why he was so sad, he told her that his father had bade his sons' wives to bake bread. The frog said, "Do not grieve, Ivan, but go to bed. Morning is wiser than evening."

In the meantime, the two sisters-in-law, who had laughed at the frog at first, now sent an old woman who worked in the kitchen to spy on the frog and see how she baked her bread. But the frog was too clever for them and guessed what they were up to. So she kneaded some dough, took off the top of the stove and threw the dough down the hole. The old woman ran to the two sisters-in-law and told them what she had seen, and they did as the frog had done.

Then the frog hopped out to the porch, turned into Vasilisa, and ordered her women and maids to make haste and set to work baking the finest soft white bread possible, the kind she had eaten in her own father's house.

In the morning, when Ivan awoke, the bread was already lying on the table, beautifully decorated with all manner of things. There were figures on the sides and towns with walls, towers and gates on the top.

Ivan was overjoyed. He wrapped the bread in an embroidered towel and took it to his father, who was just receiving the loaves his other sons had brought. Their wives had dropped the dough into the stove as the old woman had told them the frog did, and the loaves were all charred and lumpy.

The Tsar took the loaf from his eldest son and threw it away. He did the same with the bread from his middle son. But when he saw the bread which Ivan had brought, he said, "Now that is bread to be eaten only on holidays!"

Then the Tsar bade his three sons to come and feast with him on the morrow together with their wives.

Once again Tsarevich Ivan came home sad and crest-fallen. The frog hopped over the floor and came up to

him to ask him why he was so sad. Ivan told her that his father had bade the three brothers to come to a feast with their wives, and of course it would be impossible for him to bring a frog to the feast.

The frog told Ivan not to grieve but to go to the feast alone. She would follow later. When a great tramping and thundering was heard, he was not to be afraid but was to say:

"That is my Frog, riding in her carriage."

So Tsarevich Ivan went to the feast alone, and his elder brothers came with their wives, dressed in their finest clothes, with their brows blackened and roses painted on their cheeks. They all stood there and made fun of Ivan.

"Why are you here alone?" they teased. "You could have brought your wife in a handkerchief. Wherever did you find such a beauty? You must have searched all the swamps for her."

As they sat down to feast at the great tables, suddenly there was a great tramping and thundering and the palace shook and trembled. All the guests were frightened, but Tsarevich Ivan told them that they should not fear, for that was just his Frog, arriving in her carriage.

And sure enough, up to the portal of the palace came a gilded carriage, drawn by six white horses, and out of it stepped Vasilisa the Wise and Clever. Her gown was of sky-blue silk studded with stars, and on her head she wore the bright crescent moon, and so beautiful was she that it could not be pictured and could not be told, but was a true wonder to behold! She took Tsarevich Ivan by the hand and led him to the feasting tables.

The guests began eating and drinking. Vasilisa drank from her glass and poured the dregs into her left sleeve. She ate some swan meat and threw the bones into her right sleeve. The wives of the elder sons saw what she did and they did the same.

Soon the time came to dance. Vasilisa and Ivan began to dance. She danced and whirled and circled round and round, and everyone watched and marvelled. She waved her left sleeve and a lake appeared; she waved her right sleeve and white swans appeared. Everyone gasped in wonder!

Then the wives of the two elder sons began dancing. They waved their left sleeves and splashed wine dregs over the guests; they waved their right sleeves, and bones flew about on all sides, and one bone hit the Tsar in the eye. He became very angry and told the daughters-in-law to leave his sight.

In the meantime, Ivan slipped out, ran home and found the frog skin, threw it in the stove and burned it.

When Vasilisa came home and saw that her frog skin was gone, she sat down on a bench and sadly told Ivan that if he had waited but three more days, she would have been his forever. But now she would have to bid him farewell. If he wanted to see her again, he would have to seek her beyond the Thrice-Nine Lands in the Thrice-Ten Tsardom.

Saying this, Vasilisa turned into a grey bird and flew out the window.

Vasilisa arrives at the feast in the Tsar's banquet hall.

Palekh

She waved her right sleeve and white swans appeared.
(Shown actual size)

Palekh

Ivan wept and grieved for a long time. After more than a year had passed, one morning he bowed to all sides and went off, he knew not where, to seek his wife.

Whether he walked far or near, for a long time or a little time, no one knows, but his boots were worn, his caftan frayed and torn, and he was battered by the rain.

After a while, he met a little old man, who was as old as a man can be.

Ivan told the man of his troubles and the little old man said:

"Oh Ivan, why did you burn the frog skin? It was not yours to do away with. Vasilisa the Wise and Clever was born wiser and cleverer than her father, and this so angered him that he turned her into a frog for three years. But that cannot be helped now. Here is a ball of thread for you. Follow it without fear wherever it rolls."

Ivan thanked the little old man, tossed the ball of thread before him and followed where it led.

In an open field he met a bear. He took aim and was about to kill it, but the bear spoke to him in a human voice and said:

"Do not kill me, Ivan, you may have need of me some day."

Ivan took pity on the bear, and let him go. By and by he looked up and there was a drake flying overhead. Ivan took aim, but the drake also spoke to him and told him to spare him, for perhaps Ivan would have need of him some day. Ivan spared the drake and went on. Just then a hare came running. Ivan took aim quickly and was about to shoot it, but the hare also talked to him with a human voice and begged to be spared, for, said he, someday Ivan would have need of him. Ivan spared the hare and told him to be on his way.

He went further and came to the blue sea, where he saw a pike lying on the sandy shore gasping for breath. The pike begged Ivan to throw him back into the blue sea, promising that some day he would repay him for his kindness.

So Tsarevich Ivan threw the pike into the sea and walked along the shore. Whether a long time passed by or a little time, no one knows, but by and by the ball of thread rolled into a forest, and there in the forest was a little hut standing on chicken's feet, spinning round and round.

"Little hut, little hut, stand as once you stood, with your face to me and your back to the wood," said Tsarevich Ivan.

The hut turned its face to him and its back to the forest, and Ivan entered. There on the edge of the stove ledge lay the witch, Baba-Yaga, in the pose she liked best, with her crooked nose pressed up to the ceiling.

The witch asked Ivan what he wanted with her, and Ivan told her that he was seeking his wife, Vasilisa.

The witch told him that she knew where Vasilisa was, but that Koshchei the Deathless had her in his power. She told him that it would not be easy to get the better of Koshchei, for his death lay at the point of a needle, the needle was in an egg, the egg was in a duck, the duck was in a hare, and the hare was in a stone chest which was at the top of a tall oak-tree, which Koshchei the Deathless guarded fearlessly.

Ivan spent the night in Baba-Yaga's hut, and in the morning she told him where the tall oak-tree was to be found. Whether he was long on the way or not no one knows, but by and by he came to the tall oak-tree. It stood there and it rustled and swayed, and the stone chest was at the very top of it and impossible to reach.

All of a sudden, lo and behold! — the bear came running, and it pulled out the oak-tree, roots and all. Down fell the chest, and it broke open. Out of the chest bounded a hare, and away it tore as fast as it could. But another hare appeared and chased it. It caught up the first hare and tore it to bits. Out of the hare flew a duck, and it soared up to the sky. But in a thrice, the drake was upon it, and it struck the duck so hard that it dropped an egg, and the egg fell into the deep blue sea.

At this Tsarevich Ivan began to weep bitter tears, for how in the world could he find the egg at the bottom of the sea? But all at once the pike he had thrown back into the sea came swimming to the shore with the egg in its mouth.

Ivan cracked the egg, took out the needle and began to bend it to break off the point. The more he bent the needle, the more Koshchei the Deathless writhed and twisted. But all in vain, for finally Tsarevich Ivan broke off the point of the needle, and Koshchei fell dead at his feet.

Tsarevich Ivan then went to Koshchei's palace of white stone. Vasilisa ran out to him and kissed him on his mouth.

Tsarevich Ivan embraced his Vasilisa warmly and took her back with him to his own realm, where they lived together happily ever after.

Scenes from The Frog Princess. (Shown actual size)

Palekh

The Fisherman and the Magic Fish

It was a beautiful goldfish... and it spoke to him in a human voice.

(Shown actual size)

Kholui

Long, long ago, on the shore of the deep blue ocean, there lived an old man and his wife. They lived in a tumble-down hovel, and the man fished for his living. They were very poor and often had little to eat.

One day the old man cast his net in the ocean and pulled up nothing but seaweed. When he cast his net for the third time, one fish was all that he landed.

But this fish was not a common fish — it was a beautiful goldfish and as he took it gently from the net, it spoke to him in a human voice: "Put me back in the ocean, old man. If you do, I will pay you a royal ransom and give you whatever you ask of me."

The old man was astonished and frightened. He had never heard of any fish talking before. So with care he untangled the goldfish from the net and tenderly said as he did so, "God bless you, dear little goldfish! Thank you kindly, but I don't want your ransom. Go back to your home in the ocean and roam wherever you wish."

When the old man told his wife about the wondrous thing that had happened to him she started scolding, "You simpleton! He offered you a royal ransom. You at least might have asked for a wash-tub. Ours is falling apart." She scolded for so long that the old man returned to the seashore, where the blue waves were frolicking lightly, glittering in the bright sunshine. He called aloud to the goldfish, and the goldfish swam up to him and asked, "What is it, old man, what do you want?"

With a deep bow, the old man said, "Forgive me, Your Majesty Goldfish! My old woman has scolded me unmercifully. She says that she wants a new wash-tub, for ours is falling apart."

The goldfish answered him, "Do not worry, old man. Go home and you shall have a new wash-tub. God be with you."

The old man hastened home, and lo and behold, there was a new wash-tub.

But this was not enough for the old woman. She now scolded him louder and more unmercifully than ever: "Oh you simpleton, you ninny — to ask for a mere tub! Return to the goldfish, bow down low, and ask for a cottage."

Again the old man went back to the seashore and this time the blue sea was troubled. He called aloud for the goldfish and when it came to him, he bowed low and said, "Forgive me, Your Majesty Goldfish! My old woman is angrier than ever. She says that she wants a new cottage."

The goldfish murmured in answer, "Do not worry, old man. Go home and you shall have a new cottage. God be with you."

So back the old man hurried, and when he came to where his hovel had stood, he saw a beautiful new cottage with a fence around it. And there sat his old wife. When she saw him, she started to scold, louder than ever: "Oh you simpleton, you ninny. To ask for no more than a cottage! Go and bow low to the goldfish and tell it that I'm tired of being a peasant and that I want to be a fine lady!"

The old man trudged back to the seashore, where now the ocean was foaming and churning. He called out aloud for the goldfish and when it swam up to him he bowed low and said, "Forgive me, Your Majesty Goldfish! My old woman is madder than ever; she gives me no rest. She says that she is tired of being a peasant and wants to be a fine lady."

The goldfish murmured in answer, "Do not worry, old man. Go home, and God be with you."

When the old fisherman returned, he saw a wondrous sight. There stood a tall palace with white marble stairs. His old woman was wearing a rich sable jacket and a magnificent head-dress, all embroidered in gold. She had pearls on her neck and golden rings on her fingers and her feet were shod in the softest red leather. Servants bowed meekly before her. The old man approached his wife, saying, "Greetings, your ladyship, greetings, fine lady."

But she angrily bade him be silent and sent him to work in the stables.

The old woman became prouder with the passing of each day. One morning she sent for her husband and said, "Bow low to the goldfish and tell it that I am tired of being a fine lady. I want to be made a Tsaritsa."

Her husband implored her to stop asking for more than she already had, saying, "Woman, you have surely gone crazy! You can't even talk like a lady! You would be mocked by all in the kingdom."

But his old woman grew more and more angry, slapped him and shouted, "How dare you, you peasant, stand and argue with me, a fine lady? Go and do as I order at once!"

The old man went down to the seashore, and now the ocean was swollen and sullen. He called aloud for the goldfish and when it swam up to him he bowed low and said, "Forgive me, Your Majesty Goldfish! Now my old woman has gone completely crazy. She is tired of being a fine lady and wants to be made a Tsaritsa."

The goldfish murmured in answer, "Do not worry, old man. Go home and your woman will be a Tsaritsa. God be with you."

The old man hastened back and his eyes could not believe what he saw. There was a magnificent palace, and in the palace at a huge table sat his old woman, a Tsaritsa, attended by boyars and nobles who were pouring choice wines for her and filling her table with white cakes and fancy foods.

The old man was amazed and bowed low to her, saying, "Oh mighty Tsaritsa! Now I hope that your soul is contented!"

But the old lady told her chamberlains to drag him away from her presence and ordered him, under penalty of death, to keep his distance from her.

Time passed, and the old woman grew prouder than ever. One morning she sent her chamberlain to fetch her old husband from the servants' quarters. When he came before her, she said, "Go bow low to the goldfish and tell it that I'm tired of being a Tsaritsa. I wish to be mistress of all the seas and oceans, with my home in the blue ocean waters. I wish to have the goldfish for my servant to do for me everything that I command!"

The old man dared not contradict her, nor even to answer. He set out sadly for the seashore.

Now a tempest raged over the ocean. Its waters were black and angry, billowing and boiling with fury.

He called out aloud for the goldfish and when it swam up to him, he bowed low and said, "Forgive me, Your Majesty Goldfish! I do not know what to do with my cursed old woman! She is tired of being a Tsaritsa. She wants to be mistress of all the seas and oceans, with her home in the blue ocean waters. She wants you to be her own servant, to do as she commands."

The goldfish spoke not a word in answer. It just swished its tail and disappeared into the depths of the ocean in silence.

The old man waited in vain for an answer, and after many hours, he turned his steps to the palace.

Behold, instead of the palace, he saw his old hovel, and on the doorstep sat his old woman, with a broken down wash-tub at her side.

At the table sat his old woman, attended by nobles. Back view

". . . go and do as I order at once!" Front view

Palekh

(Shown actual size)

46

The Old Man and the Hares

Grandfather Mazay rescues the hares.
Kholui

(Shown actual size)

A humorous poem about an old man, Grandfather Mazay. While out hunting, he rescues hordes of hares from drowning and then warns:

But look, my friends,
Though now I free you,
When summer ends,
Don't let me see you.
I'll raise my gun,
Your day is done!

Alyonushka

Alyonushka and the little goat stand at the shore of the golden lake.   Fedoskino

Long, long ago there were two orphans, Alyonushka and her little brother Ivanushka. Their parents had died, leaving them all alone.

One fine day, the two set off from home to see the wide world.

They walked and walked until they were very tired. It was hot, and they were very thirsty, but there was no well in sight and no one to give them water.

"I am very thirsty, sister Alyonushka," Ivanushka said.

"Just be patient, little brother, we are sure to find a well soon," she answered.

On they walked until they finally came to a small pond. Nearby a herd of cows was grazing.

"Oh, there is water, sister. I will drink the water from the pond."

"No, no, little brother, if you drink water from that pond you will turn into a calf," she answered.

There was nothing to be done, so they walked on again. By and by they came to a river near which a herd of horses was grazing.

"I am so very thirsty, dear sister. Can't I have some water from the river?" asked Ivanushka.

"No, little brother, for it you do, you will turn into a colt," she answered.

Ivanushka sighed, but what could he do? They walked on and on, and by and by came to a lake, all golden in the sunset, near which a flock of goats was grazing.

48

"I am so very thirsty that I just cannot bear it any longer, dear sister. I really must have some lake water," Ivanushka exclaimed.

"Don't little brother, for if you do you will turn into a baby goat."

But Ivanushka did not listen to his sister, and when she walked ahead of him, he drank some water from the lake. The minute he swallowed the first drop, he turned into a little goat. When Alyonushka glanced back, instead of her brother, there was a little goat.

Alyonushka sat down by the lake and burst into tears. But the little goat skipped around her, and after a while she dried her eyes, tied her silken scarf around the little goat's neck, and led him off with her.

One day, the little goat happened to run into the magnificent garden of the great Tsar, and Alyonushka ran in after him. The Tsar's servants saw them, and they told the Tsar about the lovely maiden Alyonushka, who was more beautiful than anyone could ever describe.

The Tsar bade them find out who she was and bring her and her little goat into the palace. When this was done, the Tsar saw that Alyonushka was indeed as beautiful as she had been described. He fell in love with her at first sight and decided to marry her.

"Be my wife, pretty maid," said the great Tsar. "I will dress you in jewels and silks, gold and silver, and I will take good care of your little goat as well."

Alyonushka agreed to marry the Tsar, and since they did not have to wait until food was made nor wine either, as the Tsar had plenty of both in his cellars, they were married then and there. They settled down happily in the palace, and the little goat lived with them and shared their food and their drink.

One day, while the Tsar was out hunting, an evil witch suddenly appeared in the palace. She spoke sweetly to Alyonushka and lured her to the sea, where suddenly she tied a heavy stone around her neck and pushed her into the water. After that she took on Alyonushka's shape, dressed herself in Alyonushka's clothes, and went back to the palace in her stead.

As she walked into the palace grounds, the flowers in the beautiful garden wilted and the trees dried out, but of course no one guessed who she was, not even the Tsar himself. Only the little goat knew what had happened. He was sad and grieved, would not eat or drink and could not be persuaded to leave the shore of the sea, which made the witch very angry.

"Have the little goat killed," she said to the Tsar. "I am sick and tired of him."

The Tsar knew how much his wife had loved the little goat and was very perplexed at this behavior, but the witch kept coaxing and wheedling him to kill the goat, so at last he gave in.

The wicked witch ordered fires made and huge pots of water heated. She also ordered big knives to be sharpened to kill the goat.

Palekh

Alyonushka and Ivanushka set out to see the wide world.

(Shown actual size)

Alyonushka and Ivanushka.   *Mstera*

(Shown actual size)

Learning that he did not have long to live, the little goat ran to the Tsar and said, "Please, great Tsar, let me go to the shore of the sea and have a last drink of water."

The Tsar let him go and the little goat ran to the sea, stood on the shore and in piteous tones called out:

"Alyonushka, dear sister Alyonushka!
 Swim out to me, my dear sister.
 They are making huge fires.
 Pots of water are boiling.
 Great knives are being sharpened.
 The witch is going to kill me."

Alyonushka answered from the sea:

"Ivanushka, dear brother Ivanushka!
 I cannot come to you.
 There is a heavy stone pressing down on me.
 Silken weeds entangle my legs."

The little goat burst into tears and woefully went back to the palace.

By and by he again said to the Tsar, "Please, great Tsar, let me go to the shore of the sea and have a last drink of water."

The Tsar let him go, and the little goat ran back to the sea, stood on the shore and called out again in piteous tones:

"Alyonushka, dear sister Alyonushka!
 Swim out to me, dear sister.
 The witch means to kill me."

And once more Alyonushka answered from the sea:

"Ivanushka, dear brother Ivanushka!
 I cannot come to you.
 A heavy stone presses down on me.
 Silken weeds entangle my legs."

The little goat burst into tears once more and again woefully went back to the palace.

By and by he said to the Tsar for the third time, "Please, great Tsar, do let me go to the shore of the sea and have a last drink of water."

The Tsar let him go and, puzzled by the little goat's strange requests, set out to follow him.

It was almost evening when they came to the shore of the sea, and the sun turned the sea to gold. The Tsar heard the little goat call out in piteous tones:

"Alyonushka, sister Alyonushka!
 Swim out to me, dear sister.
 The witch means to kill me."

And Alyonushka answered from the sea as she had before:

"Ivanushka, dear brother Ivanushka!
 I cannot come to you.
 A heavy stone presses down on me.
 Silken weeds entangle my legs."

But the little goat went on calling her and calling her, in tones so forlorn and pitiful that at last Alyonushka could not help herself and, with superhuman strength, disentangled herself and swam out to him.

The Tsar, who was close by, ran up to her and, tearing the heavy stone away from her neck, carried her up onto the shore.

Alyonushka told the Tsar about all that had transpired. He was beside himself with joy at having her back again.

They set out for the palace together, the little goat running ahead of them and skipping happily about, and when they stepped into the garden the flowers immediately started to bloom again. The little goat turned three somersaults and lo and behold — the goat became a boy again!

They entered the palace and the Tsar ordered the witch to be put to death. She was burned in the very fires which she had had kindled for the little goat, and so that nothing could ever be left of the wicked witch, not even a memory, her ashes were thrown far out to be blown away by the wind.

The Tsar and Alyonushka lived in joy and happiness for many, many years and never had cause to shed another tear. Brother Ivanushka lived with them and shared in their happiness.

The three of them walked often at sunset by the golden sea where Alyonushka had been returned to her beloved husband.

Fedoskino

Alyonushka and Ivanushka. (Shown actual size)

Snegurochka
The Snowmaiden

There was little Snegurochka.   *Fedoskino*

Rimsky-Korsakov's opera *Snegurochka* is based on this lovely "Legend of Springtime."

Long years ago, Faerie Spring and Mighty Winter were lovers. Although their love faded and died, they were bound together by the child that was born to them, the lovely Snegurochka.

When Snegurochka was sixteen years old, her parents realized that she could no longer be hidden away and protected by them in their home in the icy North. The time had come for them to leave and bring the end of Winter and beginning of Spring to the world, and they feared that while they were gone the sun-god Yarilo would glimpse their daughter and cause her death. They went to the Spirit of the Wood, who promised that he would guard her from all harm. Her parents left to make the long preparation for Spring, and Snegurochka was allowed to go into the world, after being warned by the

Her eyes shone like crystals . . . and a jewelled crown sparkled on her head.
(Shown actual size)

Kholui

Spirit of the Wood that she was safe from death by the sun's rays only so long as love for a man did not enter her heart.

In a village in the Kingdom of Berendey, there lived an old peasant and his wife. They were very poor, but the greatest unhappiness of their lives was not their poverty but the fact that they did not have any children. They longed and prayed for a child, but their prayers were never answered.

One cold and frosty morning they went outside their cottage and lo and behold! standing there was beautiful Snegurochka! Her eyes shone like crystals and she was dressed in silken raiment; there were soft leather boots on her feet and a jewelled crown sparkled on her head. When she spoke to them they thought that they were dreaming.

"Do not be frightened," she said to them. "I have come to you to be your daughter."

The old folks were overjoyed and led her into their cottage.

After some time passed, the two old people began to notice that Snegurochka never went outdoors. They had never been as happy as they were now with this beautiful maiden in their home, for she was as respectful and kind as ever they had dreamed a daughter could be. However, they worried because she was so pale and wan, and they constantly urged her to go outdoors and walk to the village to make friends with young people of her own age.

But Snegurochka refused to go out of the cottage, telling them that she was happy to stay indoors with them. Actually, she feared going anywhere the Sun would see her.

Late one day, however, when the street in front of her cottage was filled with merry young people on their way to the village, Snegurochka watched them from inside her frosty windows, and suddenly she could no longer resist the urge to go out and be with them. She was lonely and they seemed so happy! So she put on her little cape and went out to join them.

52

On the way to the village she met a young maiden named Coupava. She was a beautiful, boisterous girl who flirted with all the lads and led a carefree existence. Coupava introduced Snegurochka to her friends, and from then on she went out from time to time in the twilight hours, to watch her new friends dance and sing.

Lel, a shepherd boy, fell in love with Snegurochka, and she felt a strange new happiness and joy whenever she was with him. They became fast friends and would often stroll and talk together.

One day a rich young merchant, Mizgir, came to the village and joined the youths and maids in their dancing. He was immediately smitten by the beautiful dark-haired Coupava, and within a few days they were lovers. He showered her with gifts of jewels and clothing, which Coupava flaunted before all the villagers.

One evening Mizgir saw Snegurochka, and from that time on his interest in Coupava waned. Now he found her too loud and bold for his taste in comparison with Snegurochka's shy and fragile beauty. He stopped seeing Coupava, and it was rumored in the village that he had begun to visit Snegurochka's home and had asked for her hand in marriage.

When Coupava heard this, she was furious! She went to Snegurochka's cottage and made a terrible scene, after which she went to the Tsar and told him that Snegurochka had enticed Mizgir away from her. She begged the Tsar to have Snegurochka punished for her wicked behavior.

The Tsar of Berendey was a mighty but benevolent ruler who always had the good of his subjects at heart. He listened attentively to Coupava and then ordered that Snegurochka be brought to him so that he could ascertain the truth of the accusations against her.

The Tsar's men came to fetch Snegurochka. Her parents were very fearful and decided to accompany her to the palace so that no harm would come to her.

When they entered the palace grounds, they were dazzled by the splendor of the scenes which greeted them. The gardens in front of the white marble palace were filled with flowering trees and shrubs of unimaginable variety. In the throne room, the ceiling and walls were covered by beautiful paintings, and precious objects were on display everywhere. Lords and boyars, dressed in furs and brocaded silks, sat on benches surrounding the Tsar. The Tsar himself sat on his bejewelled throne, dressed more magnificently than any of his lords!

Snegurochka was so overcome in the presence of the mighty monarch that she did not dare to even lift her eyes to look upon him. The Tsar told the little maiden not to be fearful, but to answer him truthfully. He explained that he had ordered her to be brought to him to find out if she had willfully stolen the heart of Coupava's lover, knowing that they were betrothed.

Snegurochka answered that, although Mizgir had indeed asked for her hand in marriage, she had refused all of his advances. The Tsar realized that the girl was speaking the truth.

"I see that this is all no fault of yours, Snegurochka. Therefore have no fear — go home now with your parents."

Kholui

He was captivated by Snegurochka's shy and fragile beauty.
(Shown actual size)

Snegurochka went home with the old couple, but from that day on she no longer went out to stroll and talk with the young people. Even Lel, her loving companion, could not persuade her to leave her cottage.

Spring finally came to the village. The sun warmed the ground, the birds returned, and the trees and flowers began to bud. The young people went to the forest to gather mushrooms and dance together. Lel came to her window often and begged her to join them, but in vain. As it grew warmer, Snegurochka became sadder and paler.

One beautiful, sunshiny day Lel came to her window and pleaded longingly for her to come out with him. Again she refused, but finally she could resist no longer. She came out of her cottage and walked with him toward the forest.

When they reached a lovely glade, Snegurochka said to him:

"Play for me, dearest friend. Play one last song for me, Lel!"

Lel took out his flute and began to play the haunting refrain which was Snegurochka's favorite tune. As she gazed upon him, love for Lel filled every fiber of her being, and she knew that this was the emotion that she had been warned against by the Spirit of the Wood. Great tears welled up in her eyes — and suddenly she began to melt!

In a few moments she had vanished completely and there was nothing left of her but a wisp of white mist which lifted slowly toward the heavens.

And so the fears of her mother had materialized. Snegurochka, the lovely daughter of Spring and Winter, had fallen in love, and Yarilo the sun-god had touched her with his warmth and claimed her for his own.

Snegurochka watched her friends dance and sing.

Palekh

54

Morozko
Father Frost and the Maiden

Morozko and Father Frost.   Mstera

Once upon a time, there lived an old man and an old woman, who had one lovely daughter. The old woman died, and shortly afterwards the old man, not being able to take care of himself or his daughter, married a woman who had a daughter of her own.

While she petted her own ugly daughter, she found fault with everything the stepdaughter did and made her work long and hard.

The old man's daughter rose before daybreak to look after the cattle, she brought the firewood and water into the house, she lit the stove and swept and scrubbed the floors. But still her stepmother scolded her all day long. Finally, one cold wintry day, the stepmother made up her mind that she would get rid of the girl for once and for all.

She told her husband to take the girl away, since she could not bear the sight of her any longer.

"Take her to the forest into the biting frost and leave her there," she said to the old man.

The old man wept and sorrowed but he knew he could do nothing, for his new wife always had her way. So he harnessed his horse and called to his daughter, "Come, my dear child, get into the sledge."

He took the girl to the forest, left her in a snowdrift beneath a large fir-tree and sadly drove away.

It was very cold, and the girl sat under the fir-tree and shivered. Suddenly, she heard Father Frost nearby, leaping from tree to tree and crackling and snapping among the twigs. In a twinkling he was on the top of the very tree beneath which she sat.

"Are you warm, my lass?" he called out to her.

"Yes, I'm very warm, dear Father Frost," she answered.

55

Father Frost came down low and he crackled and snapped louder than ever.

"Are you warm, my lass?" he called again. "Are you warm, my pretty one?"

The girl was scarcely able to take her breath, but she did not want to insult Father Frost, so she said:

"Yes, I'm very warm, dear Father Frost!"

Father Frost came down still lower, crackling and snapping very loudly indeed.

"Are you warm, my lass, my pretty sweet one?"

The girl was growing numb and could hardly move her tongue, but she said again:

"I'm very warm, good Father Frost!"

Now Father Frost took pity on the girl and wrapped her in fluffy furs and downy quilts.

Meanwhile, back in the hut, the old woman bade the old man go into the forest to bring back the body of his daughter.

The old man went to the forest and there, in the very spot where he had left her, sat his daughter, very gay and rosy. She was wrapped in a sable coat and clad in silver and gold. Beside her stood a large casket full of costly jewels.

The old man was overjoyed. He seated his daughter in the sledge, put the casket in beside her and drove home.

When the old man brought his daughter home, dazzling in her attire of furs and silver and gold, the old woman looked at her in amazement.

"Harness the horse, you old man," she said to her husband, "take my daughter to the forest and leave her in the same place as you left yours."

The old man put the old woman's daughter in the sledge, took her to the forest to the same place, left her in the same snowdrift underneath the tall fir-tree and drove away.

The old woman's daughter sat there until her teeth chattered.

By and by Father Frost came leaping from tree to tree, crackling and snapping among the twigs and stopping now and then to glance at the old woman's daughter.

"Are you warm, my lass?" he called to her.

"Oh no," said she, "I'm numb all over. Go away, you terrible old man, go away!"

Then Father Frost came down still lower and he crackled and snapped even louder and his breath grew colder and colder.

"Are you warm, my lass?" he called again.

"Oh no," she cried out. "I'm frozen! A plague on you, you miserable old Frost. I hope that the earth swallows you!"

Father Frost was so angered by these words that he gripped her with all his might and froze the old woman's daughter to death.

The dawn had hardly broken in the sky, when the old woman woke her husband and scolded:

"Make haste, you miserable old man, harness the horse and go and bring back my daughter, clad in furs and gold and silver. And make sure that the casket full of jewels is not disturbed on the trip back!"

In a little while, the gate to the cottage creaked and the old woman rushed out to greet her daughter. She turned back the cover of the sledge and there lay her daughter, quite frozen and dead.

The old woman began to scream and cry and berate her husband, but it was all to no avail.

The old man left the old woman and took his daughter to the village, where he sold the jewels for a handsome price. And so they were able to live in comfort until beautiful Morozko married a rich merchant with whom she lived happily for many years.

Beside her stood a casket full of costly jewels.

Fedoskino

Father Frost wrapped her in fluffy furs.

Palekh

(Shown actual size)

Prince Igor

Prince Igor. (Shown actual size)   *Kholui*

In spite of an eclipse of the sun, which all his subjects regard as an evil omen, Prince Igor and his son Vladimir depart for the battle against the Tatars. After they leave, Igor's beloved wife, Yaroslavna, goes to the top of the highest tower in the palace and entreats the Sun to watch over her husband.

Time passes and news comes to Yaroslavna that her husband and son have been defeated in battle and are prisoners of the Tatar leader, the great Khan Kontchak. She despairs of ever seeing Prince Igor again.

While he and his father are prisoners, Vladimir meets the beautiful daughter of the Khan, Kontchakovna, and they fall madly in love. They entreat the Khan to allow them to marry.

Although Khan Kontchak is the sworn enemy of Prince Igor, he has great respect for him both as a worthy adversary and a great warrior. Now the prospect of the union of their children puts yet another facet on the relationship of the two leaders.

Khan Kontchak orders a great feast and lavishly entertains his prisoners with food, drink and beautiful dancing maidens. When the festivities are at their height, the Khan offers Igor his freedom and great riches if he will promise never again to mount a campaign against the Tatars. Prince Igor answers that he cannot make this promise in good faith, for he feels that it is his destiny to overcome the Tatars and to defeat them for all time!

The entertainment turns into a revelry in which the entire camp becomes involved. Igor discovers his guards are asleep in a drunken stupor outside his tent and seizes this opportunity to escape. He beseeches his son to come with him, but Vladimir refuses to flee, telling his father that he will remain with the Tatars and marry Kontchakovna.

Just as dawn is breaking, Prince Igor effects his escape from the camp and returns to his subjects and to his faithful Yaroslavna, who is beside herself with joy at seeing him again.

Igor vows that when next they meet it will be he, Prince Igor, who will be victorious over the Great Khan.

In the twelfth century, Sviatoslav, the Prince of Kiev, drove the Polovtsy, a Tatar tribe from Central Asia, to the plains of the Don River and saved his kingdom from their furious onslaughts.

A generation later, the Tatars again threaten Russ and the Kingdom of Seversk, now ruled by Sviatoslav's son, Prince Igor.

The opera *Prince Igor* was composed by Borodin; the libretto for the opera was written by the composer after a play by V. Stassov, which was based on this ancient legend. Borodin died before finishing the opera, which was completed by Rimsky-Korsakov and Glazunov.

Sadko

Sadko sings at the shore of Lake Ilmen.

Kholui

Sadko is an opera by Rimsky-Korsakov based on a text by the composer and V.I. Bielsky.

The merchants of Novgorod, rejoicing in their self-importance and prosperity, are feasting in their great hall. They listen to a song sung by Nejata, a famous singer from Kiev, who accompanies himself on the *Gusli.* Nejata's song tells them of the heroic deeds of those who made Kiev a great city. Sadko, who is himself a wondrous singer, comes into the hall, and the merchants ask him to sing for them. However, his song does not please them, for in it he tells them that since Novgorod is on a lake, unless they can find some way to reach the ocean, they cannot think of bringing back to their city the marvelous fortunes which could be theirs from all over the world.

The merchants laugh at him and tell him to leave them.

Sadko goes to the shores of Lake Ilmen and sings of his despair for his beloved city. The swans on the lake are so charmed by his song that they swim towards him, and as they reach his side they turn into beautiful girls. Volkhova, the Sea Princess, is one of the young women, and she tells him that his sweet voice has made her fall in love with him. She stays with him until dawn, and when she leaves him she tells him that he will catch three golden fish in the lake that day and that he will travel to a far distant land. She promises that she will wait for his return and goes back into the water to the kingdom of her father, the King of the Ocean.

In the morning, Sadko returns to his wife, Lubava, who is devastated because of his unexplained absence. He assures her of his love for her but, mindful of Volkhova's prophesy that he will travel to a distant land, he immediately leaves his home again.

On the shore of Lake Ilmen, Sadko meets the polulace, which is crowding around the ships of the rich foreign merchant-sailors. He tells the people that golden fish can be caught in the lake. When they laugh at him, he tells them that he will wager his life against the wealth of everyone there if this is not true. A net is placed in the water, and when it is drawn up, there are gold fish in the net. Sadko has won his wager, but he does not take anything from the merchants except their ships. He asks the merchants to tell him about the lands they come from and, after hearing of many different places, decides to go to Venice. He asks the townspeople to take care of his wife, Lubava, and sets sail.

12 years pass and Sadko is sailing on his way home to Novgorod, laden with treasure from his long journey. However, his ships are becalmed. Sadko says that this is

The townspeople watch as Sadko catches golden fish from the lake.

Palekh

59

because they have failed to make the proper sacrifices to the King of the Ocean during the entire time they have been away. The sailors throw some treasure over the sides, but still the ships are becalmed. Sadko bids them throw wooden planks over the side. Sadko's ship sinks, and he dives into the water. As soon as he touches the water, a brisk breeze fills the sails of the ships and they sail away, leaving Sadko abandoned in the water.

Sadko falls to the bottom of the sea and finds himself in the kingdom of the King of the Ocean. Sadko sings for the King and Queen and to Volkhova, who sits by their side. They promise him Volkhova's hand in marriage, and the wedding guests begin to arrive. All the creatures of the ocean come to the marriage ceremony. Sadko sings to them, and they all join in a dance. The festivities and dancing become so frenzied that furious waves are lashed about in the oceans and numerous ships are sunk. An apparition warns them that the reign of the King of the Ocean is at an end. Volkhova and Sadko are plucked away from the scene by a flock of seagulls, who deposit them on the shore of Lake Ilmen. There Sadko sleeps by the side of Volkhova, who watches over him and sings a sweet lullaby. She kisses him quietly without waking him, bids him a sad farewell and disappears into the mist, becoming the great river Volkhova which flows from Lake Ilmen to the sea.

Lubava has been waiting for her husband the entire time he has been away. She is filled with happiness when she sees him at the shore of the lake, asleep. She awakens him, and he thinks that he has simply dreamed the entire voyage and the events of his marriage to the Princess of the Deep, Volkhova. But when he sees his fleet sailing towards him he realizes that it has not been a dream. There is now a river which joins Lake Ilmen to the sea, and with the treasure contained in his ships he is now the richest man in Novgorod.

All the townspeople come to the shore to greet and welcome him, and he and his wife live in comfort for the rest of their lives.

(Shown actual size)

Sadko finds himself in the Kingdom of the King of the Ocean.   *Palekh*

60

The Girl with the Golden Hair

In times before remembrance, there was once a great wizard, Poloza, who owned all the riches of the Ural Mountains. All the gold, silver and precious jewels which abounded there were guarded zealously by the magician. However, the most precious of all his possessions was his daughter, the Girl with the Golden Hair, whom he guarded even more fanatically than any of his riches. Her beauty was beyond description.

A handsome young Bashkir hunter saw the maiden and fell madly in love with her. He asked her to marry him and go to his home to live, but although she loved him too, she said that her father would never let her go.

The young hunter found a way to abduct her, but twice the magnetic power of her father made her return. On the third time, however, he was successful, for he found a place where Poloza's power was impotent. The owl had told them that if they went to a certain large island in the middle of the lake, Poloza would be powerless to touch them. But once they were there, there was no way back, so they had to be prepared to stay there forever!

The hunter and the maiden went to the island in the middle of the lake. There they found meadows and forests, herds of horses with mighty stallions, sheep, beautiful gardens, both for food and for flowers, and all manner of comforts. Poloza could not touch them

At dawn the maiden sits on a stone and lets down her golden hair.

Kholui

as long as they lived there, and they spent their days in love and happiness.

The old ones say that at dawn the maiden comes out of her home and sits on a stone at the water's edge. She lets down her long golden hair and it floats in the water and twines around the stone.

Wherever her hair touches the water, pure gold appears!

A story by Pavel Petrovich Bazhov, a contemporary poet who has written many tales dealing with the legends of the exotic Ural Mountain region.

61

The Stone Flower

Many years ago, in a village in the Ural Mountains, there lived a master stone cutter named Prokopitch. He was famous throughout the kingdom for the beauty of his work, which could not be matched by any other craftsman in the realm.

One day a young boy, Danilo, came to his workshop and said that he wanted to work with him. The boy was an orphan, who looked as though he had not eaten in days. Prokopitch took pity on him and allowed him to stay, telling him that he could do some of the menial work in the shop and live with him. Slowly Prokopitch began to teach the boy the art of stone cutting, and before much time passed he realized that Danilo had a talent that was even greater than his own. In time Danilo left the work of apprenticeship far behind and began to work together with Prokopitch on the most delicate and beautiful of the pieces being made in the workshop. As the two became engrossed in working together, their relationship took on a very different meaning; they became more father and son than master and worker.

Years passed, and Danilo grew into a handsome young man. Prokopitch, who loved him dearly, urged him to marry and start his own family, but Danilo could not find anyone to his liking. One day Prokopitch brought a lovely young maiden from the village to his home to meet Danilo. As soon as the two young people saw each other they immediately fell in love. And so, to Prokopitch's delight, Katya and Danilo were married.

An order came to the workshop from a lord of the realm for a magnificent stone cup which he wished to present to the Tsar. Prokopitch and Danilo discussed the project and it was decided that Danilo would carve the cup in the form of a stone flower. He worked on it for many weeks, but try as he would it did not come out as he wanted it to.

Danilo brooded and brooded about the cup, and finally he went to an ancient man in the village to seek advice. The old one told him that the most beautiful stone flowers in the world were in the jewelled gardens of the Mistress of Copper Mountain.

Danilo could not rest. He decided that he had to try to find the Mistress of Copper Mountain and see the stone flowers for himself. He went to the mountain and found an entrance to a cave which led to other caves. He wandered in these caverns for days until he happened upon a narrow entrance which led to still another cavern. When he entered this last cavern, the sight which greeted him was beyond human ability to describe!

Danilo stayed with the Mistress of Copper Mountain while Katya waited for his return.

Kholui

Another of the tales by Bazhov based on the legends of the Ural Mountain Region.

The walls of the huge cavern were pure malachite, and carved and jewelled flowers of all description covered the floor in all directions! The jewels sparkled so magnificently that they lit up the darkness of the cavern, and there was a magical tinkling sound as invisible currents of air made the delicate stone leaves and flowers gently brush against each other.

As he stood gazing upon this garden of riches, the Mistress of Copper Mountain appeared before him. Her beauty made even the jewels fade in comparison. Her garments were embroidered with gems of all colors, her eyes sparkled, and her hair was crowned with a diadem of precious stones. Danilo was entranced at the sight of her supernatural beauty!

She spoke to him and told him that she knew of his great talent and wished him to remain with her so that she could teach him the secrets of all the precious stones. Danilo, possessed by a strange excitement, readily agreed to stay with her.

Many months passed. Back in the village, Katya prayed for Danilo's return, but when he did not come back her family and friends urged her to marry again. She refused, for she believed that her love would bring him back to her.

One day Katya found a magnificent piece of malachite on the workroom table and felt in her heart that it was Danilo who had sent it to her. Knowing that he had gone to find the Mistress of Copper Mountain, she decided to follow him to the mountain and try to find him.

Katya entered the same cave as Danilo had, and after days of wandering she also found the entrance to the Malachite Garden. In a short time, the Mistress of Copper Mountain appeared, and Katya poured out her grief and sorrow. The Mistress was moved by Katya's expressions of love for her husband and summoned Danilo to her presence. As soon as Danilo saw Katya all the human feelings which had lain dormant in him for so long reappeared. He was overjoyed at seeing his wife.

The Mistress of Copper Mountain realized then that she could not keep Danilo with her for much longer for she was, after all, a malachite woman, incapable of returning human love. She asked Danilo if he wished to remain with her or return to Katya and his life in the village. Danilo replied that although he would always love her and be thankful for what she had taught him, it was time for him to resume his life with his wife.

When the reunited couple bid her farewell, the Mistress of Copper Mountain gave them an exquisite malachite box filled with precious jewels, which she told them to keep always.

Katya and Danilo returned to their home. They had many children and lived happily together. The children often looked at the cherished malachite box with its precious contents while their parents told them the story of the magical stone flower garden.

Danilo taught his sons the secrets that he had learned from the Mistress of Copper Mountain about the carving of precious stones, and he and his descendants were the only ones in the kingdom who could ever carve precious stones into flowers that looked as though they were truly alive.

Fedoskino

The Mistress of Copper Mountain gave them a malachite box filled with precious jewels.
(Shown actual size)

Fedoskino

Katya and the malachite box.
(Shown actual size)

The Golden Cockerel
Le Coq d'Or

The cockerel was placed on a pole on the highest tower in the palace.

(Shown actual size)

Mstera

In a faraway realm there lived a great and mighty Tsar, Dodon by name. In his prime, he was fierce and bold, and no neighboring kingdom dared to challange him, for there was no beating him at war.

As time went on, the aging Tsar became weary of fighting and felt that he had earned a rest from battle. Once his neighbors saw that he was no longer the mighty warrior that he had been in the past, they began to harass him and make quick surprise forays into his kingdom.

Dodon kept up a large army to the south and to the east and on the shores of his kingdom which successfully repelled these forays, but he was sorely vexed and tried to find some way to put an end to the constant trouble. He consulted his sons, but was not satisfied with the advice that they gave. He then called his court Astrologer to ask him for advice and help.

The old Astrologer came to the court, and with him he brought a golden cockerel. He instructed Dodon to place the cockerel on a pole on the highest tower of the land, with a clear view of all the surrounding countryside.

"The cockerel will protect thee, great Dodon,
For when there is no sign of trouble,
He will sit serene and quiet.
But should there be a threat, from any quarter,
He will crow and give full warning."

Dodon promised the Astrologer that he would give him gold and any wish that he desired at any time if indeed the cockerel would protect him from his enemies. He instructed his courtiers that the golden cockerel was immediately to be placed as the Astrologer had directed.

Time went on, and the cockerel sat on his perch. When the slightest sign of danger to the realm appeared from afar, the cockerel would ruffle up his feathers and crow, turning to the direction from which the danger came, giving the armies of Dodon plenty of time to surprise and fend off the intruders before they could come near to his kingdom.

A year passed, and Dodon's neighbors, realizing that they could never mount a surprise attack, stopped trying to seek any quarrels with him.

The libretto for the opera *Le Coq d'Or*, by Rimsky-Korsakov, is based on the poem by Alexander Pushkin.

64

Peace reigned in Dodon's kingdom for two years. The cockerel sat quietly on his perch.

One day a captain of his army rushed into his chamber to wake him and inform him that the entire city was terrified because the cockerel was crowing and violently pointing toward the east.

The Tsar instructed his oldest son to take his army to the east. The cockerel stopped his crowing.

Eight days passed, but there was no news from the army, either good or bad. Had they fought? There was no word for Dodon.

On the ninth day, the cock crowed, again pointing toward the east, and this time the Tsar sent his younger son to the east to the rescue of his brother. After this army left, the cock became quiet again.

Another eight days passed, and when there was no news of either of the two armies, a third army set forth toward the east, this time led by Dodon himself.

They marched day and night, but found no sign of the armies led by his sons. On the eighth day, Tsar Dodon ascended a hill with his men and before him in the valley between two mountain peaks was an incredible sight: A magnificent silk tent stood there, and in a ravine lay the slaughtered armies. The old Tsar and his men hastened to the scene and there before the tent, to his despair, were his two sons, each with a sword in his heart.

As Dodon and his army gave a mighty roar of grief, the silken curtains of the tent parted and there stood the young Queen of Shamakha in all her glory!

Dodon was so overwhelmed at the beauty of the Queen that all thoughts of his sons and his kingdom left his mind. The Queen of Shamakha brought the Tsar into her tent, fed him royally and led him to a gold-brocaded couch, shaded by silken curtains.

The cockerel was crowing and violently pointing to the east.

Kholui

. . . the silken curtains parted and there stood the Queen of Shamakha.

Palekh

65

Seven days and seven nights Dodon stayed with the Queen. He was completely bewitched by her beauty!

On the eighth day, Dodon declared to the Queen that he had to return to his kingdom and that she must return with him. They mounted Dodon's golden coach.

Long before they arrived at the palace, people lined the roads, for rumors of Dodon's return flew before him. As they approached the palace gates, the Astrologer appeared and welcomed the Tsar. The Tsar asked him what he wanted and the Astrologer reminded Dodon of his promise.

"What is your desire, Astrologer?" asked the Tsar.

"'Tis the maiden I wish, the Shamakhan Queen," replied the Astrologer.

The Tsar told him that he would never relinquish the Queen. He offered him gold, jewels, his best horses, half his tsardom, but the Astrologer insisted that he wanted nothing but the beautiful Queen, and that Dodon was bound by his promise to grant his wish.

Dodon became enraged and told him that he would get nothing at all. With this, he stood up and gave the Astrologer a mighty blow on the head with his sceptre, whereupon he fell dead before him.

Suddenly the golden cockerel flew down to the carriage from his perch atop the tower, flapped his wings, struck the Tsar on the top of his head with his beak and soared away. Dodon stood up, groaned once, and fell dead at the feet of the Queen.

And the Queen of Shamakha? She disappeared and was seen no more. It was as though she had never been there at all.

Scenes from The Golden Cockerel.   Palekh

(Shown actual size)

The Merchant-Peddlers

All my teasures I'll display . . .
(Shown actual size)

Fedoskino

A long poem telling of the love, life and death of a lively young peddler, Vanka, and his old companion, Tikhon. They travel many miles between villages and towns. The painting one sees most frequently on the lacquer boxes comes from the introductory passage:

> Ai! How full, how full my basket!
> Calicoes, brocades, a stack,
> Come my sweeting, make it lighter,
> Ease the doughty fellow's back.
> Steal into the rye-fields yonder,
> There till night fall I'll delay,
> When I see thy black eyes shining,
> All my treasures I'll display.
>
> I myself a heavy price paid,
> Be not chary, little dove,
> Give thy red lips, fully, freely,
> Nestle closer to thy love . . .
>
> . . . Katya bargains with discretion,
> Fears to pay too much, I ween.
> But with kisses the young fellow,
> Begs her not to be so mean.
> Well, the sombre night alone knows,
> How they managed to agree,
> Straighten up, you tall, slim rye-stalks
> Keep the secret faithfully . . .

Vanka promises Katya he will return, but after a long journey and many adventures, lengthily and penetratingly described by Nekrassov, tragedy overtakes the two pedders on their way back to her village, and Katya never sees Vanka again.

Ruslan and Ludmilla

As the mist rises ... Ruslan sees a giant Head.   Kholui
(Shown actual size)

A great feast is held in the halls of Svietosar, the Duke of Kiev, in honor of his daughter, Ludmilla. There are three suitors present at the feast who vie for her hand: Ruslan the Knight, Ratmir the poet, and Farlaf, a warrior.

When the festivities are at their height, there is a huge thunderclap, followed by darkness, during which Ludmilla mysteriously disappears.

Svietosar is distraught. He promises his daughter's hand to the suitor who can find her and bring her back to her home.

Ruslan learns from a sorcerer, Finn, that Ludmilla has been abducted by the evil dwarf Chernomor, who has magical powers and can soar through the sky with his long white beard flowing around him. He is also warned about the witch Naina, who is Farlaf's ally.

While Ruslan seeks advice from Finn, Farlaf goes to Naina for help. She tells Farlaf to allow Ruslan to go through all the trials necessary to find Ludmilla and then to simply kidnap her from Ruslan.

Ruslan's search takes him to a battlefield, enmeshed in a heavy mist. Here he finds a lance and shield. When the mist begins to clear, he sees a giant Head, which creates a mighty storm with its breath. Ruslan subdues the Head with the lance, and under the Head he finds a magic sword, which will enable him to overcome all obstacles.

The opera *Ruslan and Ludmilla* by Glinka is based on Pushkin's monumental poem, which many critics consider one of his finest works.

Ludmilla in Chernomor's garden.
(Shown actual size)

Palekh

Meanwhile, although Ludmilla is held captive in Chernomor's castle, she is given every comfort and is allowed to walk freely in the sumptuous garden behind the tall walls which surround the castle on all sides. Here she finds herself in the midst of majestic trees and a profusion of blooming flowers and blossoming shrubs. Magnificent peacocks and gentle deer walk beside her. Brilliantly colored birds are everywhere.

But Ludmilla cannot be consoled by the beauty around her. She despairs, for she fears that she will never be rescued from the evil Chernomor and returned to her home.

After vanquishing the Head, Ruslan rides to Chernomor's castle. When he arrives, Chernomor forces Ludmilla into a sleeping trance and then goes to meet the Knight in combat. Because he has the magic sword, Ruslan is victorious and carries Ludmilla away. But he cannot awaken her from her sleep.

Ruslan obtains a magic ring from Finn, and, with the aid of this ring, he breaks Chernomor's spell. The Knight brings Ludmilla back to her father's court, where they are greeted with great joy.

Ruslan and Ludmilla are married amid great festivities, and live together happily for the rest of their lives.

Ruslan at the gates of Chernomor's castle.

(Shown actual size)

Palekh

The wedding feast of Ruslan and Ludmilla.

Palekh

The Epic of Prince Igor - Kholui

(Shown actual size)

Cathedrals and Monasteries - Kholui

Ancient Monasteries of Uglich.

Ancient Monasteries of Suzdal.

Kideksha

Village of Kholui

Village of Kholui

Village of Kholui

Bell Towers of Rostov.

The "Small Miracles" of Palekh

Tsar Saltan.

Ruslan and Ludmilla.

The Frog Princess.

Tsar Saltan

Snegurochka.

(Shown actual size)

Cabinet with three drawers.
Scenes from Ruslan and Ludmilla are
painted on front, sides and top.
47 x 45 x 18 cm

from Mstera

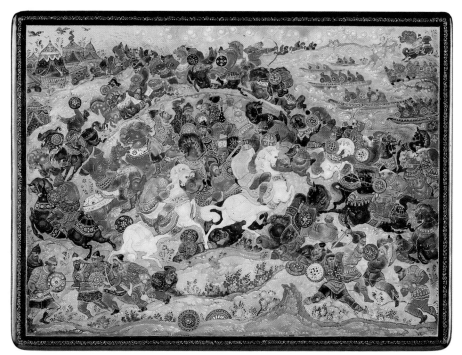

The Battle of 1223 at the Kalka River

Ruslan and Ludmilla.

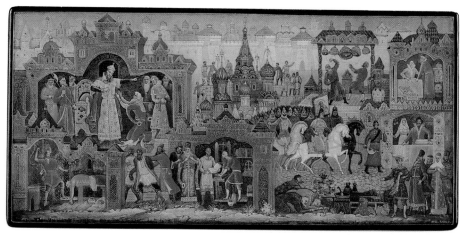

Life of Ivan the Great

The Master Builders.

Flowers.

Fedoskino

The Boyar's Wedding.   Fedoskino

Morning in the Woods.

The Rooks are Returning.

Troikas

Palekh

Fedoskino

Palekh

Palekh

Palekh

Village Life

Meeting on the way to the well. Palekh

Village Life. Palekh

Going to the well. Palekh

Picking Mushrooms. Palekh

Lovers. Palekh

Tea Party. Palekh

Bread and Salt-symbol of hospitality. Fedoskino

In the forest. Palekh

Northern Song. Fedoskino

Gossiping. Fedoskino

UNFORTUNATELY, SPACE DOES NOT PERMIT US TO LIST ALL THE DISTINGUISHED LACQUER MINIATURE PAINTERS. THE WORKS OF MANY OF THE ARTISTS LISTED BELOW ARE REPRESENTED IN MUSEUMS IN THE U.S.S.R. AND HAVE BEEN EXHIBITED THROUGHOUT THE WORLD. SOME OF THESE PAINTERS HAVE RECEIVED THE HIGHEST AWARDS IN THE FIELD OF ART THAT THEIR COUNTRY CAN BESTOW.

PALEKH:

O.V. AN

T.G. ANDRIJASHKINA

V. ABRAMOV

B. BAKANOV

R.L. BELOUSEV

Y.I. BELOZEROV

V.A. BELOZEROVA

G.P. BOGATIKOVA

V.V. BULDAKOV

N.B. BULDAKOVA

G.A. BURCHEVA

D.N. BUTORIN

A.A. DEMIDOV

A. DOCHLIGIN

V. ERMOLAEVA

V.P. FEDOROV

N.I. GOLIKOV

V.M. KHODOV

Z.A. KHOKHOV

A.D. KOCHUPALOV

V.A. KOROVKIN

A.A. KOTUKHINA

A.U. KOVALEV

V. KOZLOV

S.G. KUKULIEVA

A.M. KURKIN

G.V. KUZMENKO

A.V. KUZNETZOV

L.M. KUZNETZOV

G.N. LIATOVA

N.P. LOPATIN

G.G. MARKOVA

F.N. MELNIKOVA

V.V. MUHIN

A.O. POCHANIN

O.L. SMIRNOVA

V.A. SMIRNOV

V.F. SMIRNOVA

V.I. SMIRNOV

V.N. SMIRNOV

V. TEHERIN

I.A. VINOGRADOV

Z.I. VIUGINA

E.G. ZHIRIAKOV

G.A. ZHIRIAKOVA

L.S. ZVERKOVA

KHOLUI:

V. AKIMOV

V. BABKIN

N.I. BABURIN

V.A. BELOV

N.N. DENISOV

A.H. DOBRINYA

V.A. ELKIN

E.M. FILIPPOV

V.I. FOMIN

A.A. KAMORIN

B.I. KISELYEV

V.I. KOCHETKOV

A.M. KOSTERIN

N.N. LOPSHIN

A.K. MIAKISHEV

P.A. MITIASHIN

A.A. MOROZOV

B.K. NOVOSELEV

V.N. SEDOV

N.P. SHUBIN

A.A. SMIRNOV

FEDOSKINO:

N.P. ALDOSHKIN

V.D. ANTONOV

E. GUREEV

Y.V. GUSSEV

Y.V. KARAPAYEV

Y.P. KHOMUTINIKOV

V.A. KROTOV

G.I. LARISHEV

V.D. LEPITSKY

A.A. MOROZOV

M.G. PACHININ

P.I. PUCHAEV

N.N. SEDOV

S.D. SEDOV

I.I. STRACHOV

M.S. TCHIZHOV

MSTERA:

V. ANTONOVSKY

V. AVDEEVA

L.A. FOMECHEV

A. FROLOV

A.R. GAUN

G. GRACHEV

M.A. KULTICHOVA

V.V. KURCHATKIN

V.A. LEBEDEV

B.N. LUBOMUDROV

N.A. LUBROMUDROVA

I.O. MAXIMOV

U.F. MALACHOVA

N.V. MEDVEDEV

V.N. MOLODKIN

P.P. MOZHAIEV

V.K. MOZHKOVITCH

A.D. SHADRIN

N.I. SHISHAKOV

V.A. TIKHOMIROV

Y.M. VAVANOV

L.G. ZUIKOV

The jacket is reproduced in 7 colors. The illustrations in
this book are reproduced from original lacquer miniature
paintings on boxes, panels and plates created in Palekh, Kholui, Fedoskino
and Mstera. Art work and lay-out was designed by Von Eiff Studios, Oakdale,
New York. Photography by Van Camp Studios, Melville, New York.

Printing by Frank C. Toole & Sons, Inc., Farmingdale, New York.